A Land Like Your Own

A Land Like Your Own

Traditions of Israel and Their Reception

Edited by
JASON M. SILVERMAN

AMY DAUGHTON
Contributing Editor

☙PICKWICK *Publications* · Eugene, Oregon

A LAND LIKE YOUR OWN
Traditions of Israel and Their Reception

Copyright © 2010 Wipf and Stock Publishers. All rights reserved. Except for brief quotations in critical publications or reviews, no part of this book may be reproduced in any manner without prior written permission from the publisher. Write: Permissions, Wipf and Stock Publishers, 199 W. 8th Ave., Suite 3, Eugene, OR 97401.

Scripture quotations from the New Revised Standard Version of the Bible are copyright © 1989 by the Division of Christian Education of the National Council of the Churches of Christ in the United States of America and are used by permission.

Pickwick Publications
An Imprint of Wipf and Stock Publishers
199 W. 8th Ave., Suite 3
Eugene, OR 97401

www.wipfandstock.com

ISBN 13: 978-1-60899-454-0

Cataloging-in-Publication data:

A land like your own : traditions of Israel and their reception / edited by Jason M. Silverman; Amy Daughton, contributing editor.

xvi + 160 p. ; 23 cm. — Includes bibliographical references.

ISBN 13: 978-1-60899-454-0

1. Bible. N.T.—Relation to the Old Testament. 2. Bible—Criticism, interpretation, etc. I. Silverman, Jason M. II. Daughton, Amy. III. Title.

BS1188 L40 2010

Manufactured in the U.S.A.

ושננתם לבניך ודברת בם בשבתך בביתך ובלכתך בדרך ובשכבך ובקומך

To Professor A. D. H. Mayes.

Contents

List of Contributors / ix

List of Illustrations and Tables / x

Abbreviations / xi

Introduction—Amy Daughton and Jason M. Silverman / *xiii*

1. On Religious and Cultural Influence—*Jason M. Silverman* / 1
2. The Synagogue at Herodium: Problematic Fact or Problematic Fiction?—*Lidia D. Matassa* / 13
3. Gender and Syro-Palestinian Archaeology: A Post-Feminist Perspective—*Cynthia Shafer-Elliott* / 41
4. Reconsidering Jacob: A Gendered Approach to Genesis 25:19–34—*Trisha Tschopp* / 52
5. Of Donkeys and Witnesses: Interpolation or Interpretation?—*Giovanna Raengo Czander* / 69
6. The Influence of Egyptian Throne Names on Isaiah 9:5: A Reassessment of the Debate in Light of the Divine Designations in the Book of Isaiah—*Máire Byrne* / 87
7. Jesus and Yeshua: Jewish Interpretations of the Gospels and Its Impact on Jewish-Christian Dialogue —*Peter Admirand* / 101
8. 1 Peter as Biblical Proto-Theodicy: Reconciling Suffering Communities and Faithful Creator—*Richard I. Kueh* / 114
9. Interpreting Together and Receiving New Testament Concepts of Apostolicity—*Miriam Haar* / 132
10. Defense and Disputation, Erudition and Exchange: An Overview of the History of New Testament Translations into Hebrew—*Murray Watson* / 145

Contributors

Peter Admirand
Irish School of Ecumenics, Trinity College Dublin

Máire Byrne
Milltown Institute

Amy Daughton
Trinity College Dublin

Miriam Haar
Irish School of Ecumenics, Trinity College Dublin

Richard I. Kueh
Peterhouse, University of Cambridge

Lidia D. Matassa
Trinity College Dublin

Giovanna Raengo Czander
Dominican College

Cynthia Shafer-Elliott
University of Sheffield

Jason M. Silverman
Trinity College Dublin

Trisha Tschopp
Hebrew College, Massachusetts

Murray Watson
St. Peter's Seminary, Ontario

Illustrations and Tables

Figure 1	Religio-Cultural Influence / 6
Figure 2	Herodium Looking South from Bethlehem / 14
Figure 3	Context and Locations / 16
Figure 4	The Triclinium / 19
Figure 5	Mikveh, Triclinium, Kiln, and Water Installation / 24
Figure 6	Comparison of Locus 1042 on Masada and the Triclinium at Herodium / 32
Figure 7	Table of References to Suffering in 1 Peter / 118

Abbreviations

Ant	Josephus *Jewish Antiquities*
BDB	Brown, Francis, S. R. Driver, and Charles A. Briggs. *A Hebrew and English Lexicon of the Old Testament. Based on the Lexicon of William Gesenius as Translated by Edward Robinson.* Oxford: Clarendon, 1966
JW	Josephus *Jewish Wars*
JSOTSS	Journal for the Study of the Old Testament Supplement Series
JSNTSS	Journal for the Study of the New Testament Supplement Series

Introduction

Amy Daughton and Jason M. Silverman

> Every one of you will eat from his own vine and fig tree and drink water from his own cistern, until I come and take you to a land like your own—a land of grain and new wine, a land of bread and vineyards.
>
> Isaiah 36:16–17

Human culture and tradition is a dialectic of sameness and difference, of new work entangled with the always already present narratives and values of society and its pasts. This situation is an inescapable facet of the human condition to which one can choose to react either with fruitful refiguration or despair. While this dynamic moves in all communities, the traditions birthed by ancient Israel perhaps bear this out most spectacularly. A tiny people in a region dominated by imperial powers produced a literature that still profoundly influences the Western world. No less than three religions claim continuity with the heirs of Abraham, yet no living tradition today even approximates the religion that was practiced near the trees of Mamre. The gods of the Midianites may be forgotten, but their stories have flowed into a broad and fruitful stream that still nourishes.

Reflecting on Sennacherib's taunt to the Jerusalemites in Isaiah 36 (parallels 2 Kings 18),

> Rabbi Johanan said: Why did that evil man merit the titles of the great and noble Asnapper?—Because he did not speak slightingly of the Land of Israel, as it is written, Until I come and take you away to a land like your own land. (Babylonian Talmud, *Sanhedrin* 94a)

The Rabbis of the Talmud averred that, in that insult, even the Assyrian king understood that one's own heritage cannot be easily and lightly thrown away. Tradition is always already part of our self-creation—even when we turn it aside, we still carry its tools with us. The preposition "like" hides the dialectical razor upon which the construction and re-formulation of traditions balance; to see something as "like" means to see it as both familiar and foreign, comparable but not superior, both as hope and mourning. For Sennacherib, it was a message of hope; for the Jerusalemites, an inducement towards disloyalty to their land and their G-d; for the Rabbis, a recognition of the superiority of Israel. Yet for the exiles and their descendants, the question was what to do with this new land, like their own, confronting them. In this new space should they embrace it as their own and abandon the old land, mold it into a closer image of Israel, or let the dissimilarity nurture a longing and a hope for a kingdom irrevocably lost? Ultimately, the dialectical nature of the choice—of the "like"—allows the work of both extremes, seeking new ways of living, in continuity with one's heritage, even while mourning what might be lost in the transition. Both of these are part of "the representative function of the historical imagination. We learn to see a series of events *as* tragic, as comic, and so on,"[1] and it is by this activity, either in joyous recall or grieving farewell that the Israelites called back their land, to be present amongst them again, even in Assyria, in their stories, their ways of living, their relationship with the land.

The power of the exilic paradigm in the Hebrew Scriptures speaks directly to this situation of discordant lands and the choice each generation must make in regards to the "land," the text, bequeathed by the previous generation. Formed by that tradition, how will each person contribute to it? It is in that same movement that we are able to speak of the other, the past, and the text, *like* our self, *like* our own narratives. To so analyze is to seek similarity, while retaining a recognition of difference, of particularity. The scholarly task is to speak across that gap to the other, be it event or text or person, drawing them closer, even while allowing that other to *be* other.

While the "land" of academia may look like foreign territory to the realities of everyday life, the task done explicitly by and amongst scholars is the same kind of sifting done implicitly in other human communities.

---

1. Paul Ricoeur, *Time and Narrative III*, trans. Kathleen Blamey and David Pellauer (Chicago: Chicago University Press, 1988).

Tradition changes; understanding its implications and history can make it a source for hope and creativity instead of despair and stagnation.

All of the essays contained herein deal with the reception and refiguration of legacies, either in their initial creation or in their modern reception. While a wide variety of texts, topics, and communities are discussed, as a collection they emphasize the continuing and dialectical nature of the hermeneutical process—bound neither by community nor disciplinary scope. Within these essays the canonical scriptures and the communities of Jews and Christians repeatedly cross paths in unexpected ways, from the murky prehistory of Israel to the present day.

Finding little methodological explicitness or clarity in discussions of how communities interact, *Jason M. Silverman* offers a model for understanding how interactions between communities can be understood and suggests criteria for seeing it in literary works. *Lidia D. Matassa* examines the archaeological evidence for a first-century synagogue in Herodium, reacting to the effects of pre-existing expectations on the interpretation of material culture. *Cynthia Shafer-Elliott* explicitly takes up a critique of gender archaeology to remind scholars that the theory must serve the evidence. Gender concerns are also applied by *Trisha Tschopp* to place the Jacob and Esau narrative of Genesis in the context of folkloric traditions and to explore how gender roles can be simultaneously transgressed and upheld. Also exploring the final form of the text, *Giovanna Raengo Czander* argues that the apparent incongruity of the legal traditions of Exodus 23 is a deliberate attempt to expand the ethical demands of the law and should not be dismissed as shoddy editing. Going behind the structure of the present text, *Máire Byrne* explores the significance of names in Isa 9:5. She questions the scholarly reading of subsequent Christian history into the origin of the text, seeking historical context for the understanding of the text's original meaning. *Peter Admirand* explores how divergent interpretations of shared traditions about Jesus impact the contemporary engagement of Jews and Christians. In the New Testament, *Richard I. Kueh* uses "reception" in two complementary ways. Seeking to understand the function, context and earliest reception of 1 Peter, he explores how early Christians held in tension the received tradition of Israel's G-d with the present reality of their communities' sufferings. The need to understand received traditions affects not only inter-religious dialogue, but, as explored by *Miriam Haar*, affect intra-religious dialogue. Bringing the discussion back to the sacred texts themselves, *Murray Watson* explores the effects of languages and their translations in the reception of sacred texts.

This collection began as papers that were selected and expanded from those given at the Second and Third Annual Graduate Interdisciplinary Approaches to the Biblical World (GIA) conferences, held at Trinity College Dublin in the Februaries of 2008 and 2009. These conferences and this collection would not have been possible without the support of numerous people. Special thanks is due to the GIA organizing committee, without whom the conferences would not have transpired, and who made the experiences both academically and socially rewarding. The conference was run under the auspices of the School of Religions and Theology, Trinity College Dublin, and was generously supported by the Long Room Hub, Trinity College Dublin. Dr. Jason McElligott is to be thanked for facilitating their funding. Several scholars lent support through their encouragement and engagement, in particular Prof. Susan Niditch, Prof. A. D. H. Mayes, Dr. Anne Fitzpatrick-McKinley, and Dr. Roja Fazaeli. Ms. Jane Welsh provided invaluable logistical assistance both for the conferences and for this volume.

It is hoped that readers may see within these pages tools for refiguring the narratives of their own intellectual and spiritual homelands.

Dublin
1 November 2009

1

On Religious and Cultural Influence

Jason M. Silverman

INTRODUCTION

STUDENTS OF BIBLICAL TEXTS often encounter the question of these texts' relations to the extra-Israelite/Judaean cultures among which they lived. These relations can be understood in a number of ways, as isolationism, general regional *koine*, or influence of some kind. Since Palestine had numerous contacts with many civilizations, research often appeals to parallels with texts from Egypt, Mesopotamia, Greece, or Iran. While these kinds of studies are valuable, they are methodologically and conceptually treacherous.

To discuss questions of influence, it is first necessary to clarify what is meant by the term and to specify a working methodology for assessing its presence and effects.[1] This paper offers a model for understanding influence and offers criteria for determining its presence in texts. The term "influence" is here understood as one type of "interaction." "Interaction" here denotes a variety of types of intercourse, from superficial to significant, including the social-situational phenomenon of the meetings of cultures as well as the "intellectual" side. Political and social structures as well as cultural and religious elements are included in the concept. This

---

1. This seems to not have received much attention as a topic in and of itself. Critiques of comparative methods, however, abound. Cf. Talmon, "The 'Comparative Method' in Biblical Interpretation"; Sandmel, "Parallelomania"; Cf. Poole, "Metaphors and Maps."

is generally recognized as being nigh universal.² The scholarly use of the term for the intellectual side of interaction—"influence" or "dialogue"—is inconsistently used, however, with a variety of connotations attached. It is therefore important to note what is not meant by the word "influence" here: it does not mean a wholesale "cut and paste" of literate materials from one canon to another (say, from the *Bundahišn* to *1 Enoch*). Neither does it denote a religious conversion under another name, nor does it indicate the "syncretism" or "assimilation" of anthropologists.³ Of concern here is not the development of entirely new systems or traditions, but of change *within* a system due to external interaction; the question of how much change a system or tradition can undertake before being a new system is an interesting problem, but it cannot be broached here.⁴ Interaction and influence are here understood as unavoidable aspects of the human condition, one which has impacted and continues to impact all traditions and religions. In all cultures, and particularly in largely oral cultures, influence is a subtle affair and requires much thought to tease out.

INFLUENCE: A CONCEPTUAL MODEL

Hinnells offers a suggestive discussion of the types of influence possible between communities, and his ideas are worth keeping in mind when assessing questions of influence.⁵ He notes two basic types of influence, each with their own variations: (1) the conscious imitation or borrowing of elements from another tradition. This can be either positive (i.e., accepting ideas accepted in another tradition) or negative (i.e., rejecting ideas which are rejected in another tradition); (2) conscious rejection of another tradition. The rejection of a tradition, however, can still affect the rejector's own tradition in two ways: (a) by rejecting aspects of own tradi-

---

2. Lesser, "Social Fields and the Evolution of Society," 41; Light, "Orthosyncretism," 185; Vroom, "Syncretism and Dialogue," 109; Boyd and Richerson, *Origin and Evolution of Cultures*, 333, 421; Swadesh, "Diffusional Cumulation and Archaic Residue."

3. Anthropologists seem to be more interested in a biologically-inspired typology ("phyogenetics"); cf. Goodenough, "Phylogenetically Related cultural traditions"; Dallmayr, *Beyond Orientalism*, chap. 1; Durham, "Applications of Evolutionary Culture Theory."

4. For the purposes of discussion, "tradition" and "system" are deliberately broad: they include both overarching religions (e.g., Judaism) and more specific groups (e.g., Qumranic Judaism).

5. See Hinnells, "Zoroastrian Influence on the Judeo-Christian Tradition," 9–11.

tions seen to conform too closely to the rejected one; (b) by utilizing the modes of discourse of the rejected tradition to combat or argue with it. Hinnells notes that type 1 will often occur consciously while type 2 will often occur unconsciously, although either can simultaneously function consciously and unconsciously.[6] In addition to these forms of influence, a tradition can be influenced by using new ideas to re-interpret native ideas. This last type of influence is the most difficult to detect, because it will for the most part utilize native ideas and motifs and will claim to be an organic growth of the tradition. All of these types of influence are possible—even likely—even in situations without external coercion (such as a state-mandated reform program). In other words, an officially supported "missionary" program is not necessary for influence to occur; it can quite simply happen when two cultures interact on a personal level. This personal level includes administrative scenarios as well as scenarios from the course of everyday life.

Two studies from a slightly different scholarly debate[7] highlight two important aspects of any religious tradition: within each system there is a continual presence of hermeneutics as well as a hierarchy of importance for each element within the tradition.[8] No human is static, and individuals will continually (re-)interpret their traditions. However, in this process, elements that are considered to be more peripheral are prone to more extensive reinterpretation than those that are central. Vroom, emphasizing the incorporation of "foreign" and "incompatible" elements within a tradition, argues that such incorporation involves the reinterpretation of old beliefs as well as a reconfiguration of the relative structural importance of elements within the receiving system.[9] Without limiting the discussion to traditions that are "incompatible" as Vroom does, his observations on the results of influence or borrowing on the receiving tradition are still useful for evaluating less radical influences. The reinterpretation of elements within a system and the importation and adaption of elements into a system will necessitate the altering of the "ratios" and relations in that system. In other words, foreign influence is most likely to occur in negotiable aspects of a tradition, while still having effects beyond itself in

6. Ibid., 10.

7. The History of Religions and Anthropological debate over "Syncretism," which appears to focus on slightly different questions than the ones of interest to this study.

8. Vroom, "Syncretism and Dialogue," 103–12; Light, "Orthosyncretism," 162–85.

9. Vroom, "Syncretism and Dialogue," 109.

the system as a whole. When analyzing potential instances of influence, then, it is necessary to consider (1) areas in the receiving tradition which are most susceptible to reinterpretation (i.e., how central or peripheral they are); (2) the re-interpretation which would be needed or effected by the influence or borrowing; and (3) the relative structural impact on the receiving system.

Light understands religions to consist of three "cognitive entities": symbols, categories into which symbols are arranged, and the organizational rules which govern the importance and interactions of symbols and categories.[10] The rules that govern the relative importance or types of acceptable change will vary drastically from tradition to tradition, so that rules that are valid for one tradition will not likely be the same for another. This means that a change (or influence) which one tradition may be able to accept as normal and unproblematic could very well be "*a drastic and traumatic alteration in foundational understanding from the viewpoint of the other tradition.*"[11] This relates to Vroom's understanding of the structural importance of a given element within a tradition, and Light's illustrations make the point amply clear: while the Chinese religions are easily able to assimilate a new deity, the same is not true of the monotheistic religions. Even though two religions may share an analogous category of "divinity," they need not have the same structural importance, thus qualifying any superficial parallel between them.[12] Thus, to a Christian scholar the adoption of a new deity looks like a drastic change, while to a devotee of Chinese religion it would not. As a result, Light posits "two principles of religious syncretism": the principle of religious change and the principle of cognitive integrity.[13] These are similar to the views of Vroom noted above. Light posits that change will most likely produce a re-arranging of the structure and a redefinition of symbols within that structure, although the tradents will understand the process as simply a normal part of the hermeneutical process. Further, it is to be expected that the elements most likely to be influenced or borrowed are of less structural importance to or fit within currently existing categories of the receiving tradition. In other words, interaction will appear completely natural and organic within the

---

10. Light, "Orthosyncretism," 163.
11. Ibid., 178, emphasis his.
12. Similar to the objections put forward by Sandmel, "Parallelomania," 5, 7.
13. Light, "Orthosyncretism," 180.

adapting system, even if, from another (outside) perspective, it appears to be quite radical.

For the purposes of this study, the terms "interaction," "influence," and "borrowing" are distinguished and defined as follows. "Interaction" denotes the participation in social and intellectual intercourse with those of other religions and cultures that occurs in normal human society. This interaction can have three types of result on a culture as is visible in texts. "Borrowing" refers to the usage of a term, story, or other discrete element that is taken from another culture or religion. This is similar to, but here distinguished from, "quotation," which is reserved solely for the direct and intended reference to a text or saying. "Influence" designates the reshaping, selection, and/or interpretation of ideas, stories, characters, or doctrines from the native traditions due to interaction with another culture. As noted by Hinnells, this can be conscious or unconscious, positive or negative. These three forms of interaction are not, in practice, so easily delimited; however, it is useful to make the distinction for purposes of clarity (see Figure 1). Immediately apparent from these definitions is the fact that two types of interaction—incidences of quotation and borrowing—are the easiest to identify.[14] All four forms of influence delineated are difficult to spot, with the negative forms perhaps impossible without the aid of additional, non-textual evidence.[15] A rather intimidating amount of data would probably be needed to demonstrate the unconscious rejection of internal traditions due to similarities with another tradition, and as such it is probably not often possible for Second Temple Judaism; nevertheless, the possibility ought to be kept in mind.

Given the subtleties involved in interaction, how can its presence and effects be detected in texts, the primary remaining source of evidence for ancient civilizations and religions?

CRITERIA FOR POSITING FOREIGN INFLUENCE IN A TEXT

Barr delineates two basic approaches to comparative studies: general and specific.[16] He notes that general comparisons or lists of parallels do not

---

14. For a discussion of the problematics of identifying allusions, see Wold, *Women, Men, and Angels*, 49–78; for quotations, see Schultz, *Search for Quotation*, 109–12, 214.

15. For a discussion of these questions in the interpretation of archaeology see the thought-provoking collection in Clarke, ed., *Archaeological Perspectives on the Transmission and Transformation of Culture in the Eastern Mediterranean*.

16. Barr, "Question of Religious Influence, 204.

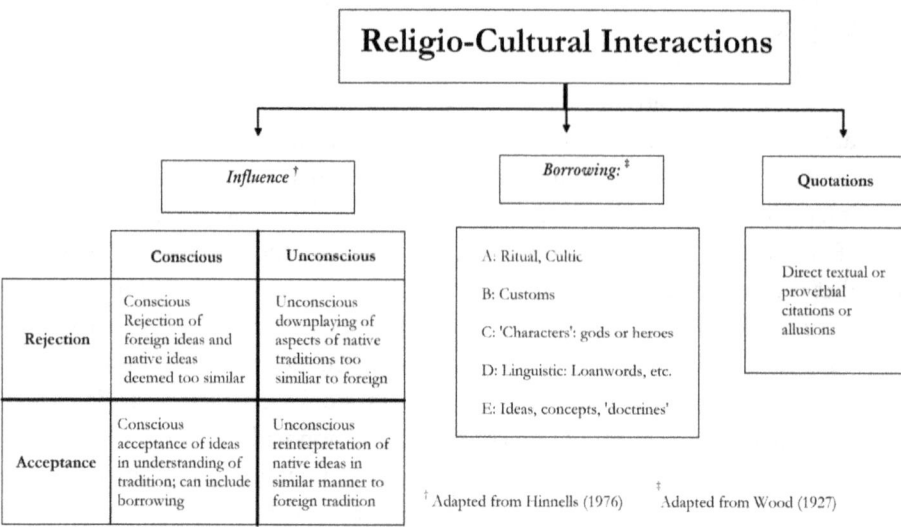

FIGURE 1: Religio-Cultural Interactions

constitute evidence of interactions; detailed, specific argument is needed to demonstrate that the general parallel is indeed not just happenstance.[17] Specifically, he emphasizes the need for explanatory circumstances and motivations which occasioned borrowing. This also needs to be undertaken with an understanding of the structural import of the proposed influence or borrowing in both source and new context. Although Barr only briefly alludes to the possibility of negative or unconscious influence,[18] his insistence that proposed parallels must be understood within the greater structural contexts is important. Rarely do people or groups adopt wholly different ideas to their own, nor do they adopt them without adaptation to their own worldview. The student must be careful to understand how a detail or concept could both be transformed by *and* transform the receiving tradition.

In broaching the question, Wood suggests five criteria that a proposed parallel must satisfy to be considered an instance of borrowing:

---

17. Ibid., 206.
18. Ibid., 208, 230.

1. Did the receiving tradition have a need that the borrowed idea fulfilled?
2. Are there similar sources in the receiving tradition which could evolve in a similar manner?
3. Did similar ideas pre-exist in the receiving tradition?
4. Could the element come from elsewhere as well?
5. Can the source tradition be reliably dated earlier?[19]

Wood's last criterion is certainly the most important; the source must predate the reception. The fourth question is also a valid concern; if similar ideas do appear in multiple contexts, one must decide whether there are enough details to justify the identification of a single source, or whether the idea is more the result of a general *Zeitgeist* and can therefore no longer be called "influence." However, the first criterion is historically dubious, depending on the intent of the question: the proper historical question is not the *necessity* but the *probability* of what did happen in the past.[20] If Wood means that there must be a "space" or way in which element can be utilized, then that is the same as the next two criteria. The second and third criteria appear to be the same criterion. For interaction to exist, there must be a "hanger" upon which the borrowed "coat" can hang in the receiving "wardrobe." People rarely adopt ideas that appear to them wholly alien.[21] Thus, Barr's concerns about the structural import in both traditions are necessary to understand the nature and likelihood of interaction.[22]

In light of the above considerations, five general criteria and one additional criterion for "influence" are here proposed. The first two criteria are really preconditions: (1) the proposed source must predate the proposed incidence of interaction; and (2) there must be a plausible historical context for the interaction. The remaining criteria are more difficult to establish or demonstrate. (3) The foreign element must make

---

19. Adapted from Wood, "Borrowing between Religions," 104–5.
20. Cf. the comment in Hinnells, "Zoroastrian Influence on the Judeo-Christian Tradition," 9.
21. "Alien" is not the same as "novel"; the criteria for an element being "alien" rather than simply novel varies greatly between individuals and systems.
22. Kraeling's proposals, besides offering similar concerns to Barr and Wood, merely add a concern for the historical particulars and scholarly consensus. Kraeling, "Method in the Study of Religious Syncretism."

more structural "sense" in the original context than in the new one. (4) There must be a "hook" or way in which the foreign element could be included in the tradition. And (5) there must be discrete, distinctive elements that betray the origin of the element. These must be more distinctive or specific than potential parallels from other sources. Any form of borrowing in a text is certainly evidence that interaction on some level has occurred, but on its own is insufficient to demonstrate the presence of influence. The accumulation of multiple, detailed borrowings certainly tilts the scales towards the possibility of influence,[23] yet a sixth criterion is needed to demonstrate influence as defined above: (6) there must be an interpretive or structural change in the receiving tradition on account of the influence. This is perhaps the most important (albeit evanescent) of the six criteria.

The first two criteria are straightforward and require no further justification. The others require more elucidation. The third criterion—the foreign element must make more structural sense in its original context—means that there should be indications that the element more "organically"[24] fits within the source tradition than in the receiving one, therefore making it more probable that its appearance in the receiving tradition is due to interaction rather than parallel internal developments. For example, the belief in the Davidic covenant in Jerusalem leads logically to the concept of the inviolability of Zion. If the same Zion doctrine were discovered in a text from a neighboring country without an analogous royal tradition, it could indicate borrowing or influence. The fourth criterion is the requirement for a "hook" or space for the new element in the receiving tradition. This is similar to Wood's insistence on the fulfilling of a need and Barr's insistence on a plausible motivation.[25] There must be a way in which the receiving tradition could have incorporated the element and still have perceived it as being consonant with said tradition (in line with Light's principle of cognitive integrity).[26] A potential example would be the adaptation of a dualism as a response to monotheistic theodicy. Since monotheistic theodicy can prompt a plethora of solutions, dual-

---

23. Provided the borrowings are of an useful nature; cf. Sandmel, "Parallelomania," 10.

24. To use the term utilized by Shaked, "Iranian Influence on Judaism," 323.

25. Cf. Wood, "Borrowing between Religions," 104; Barr, "Question of Religious Influence," 206.

26. Light, "Orthosyncretism," 180.

ism can easily be understood as one such "internal" response. The fifth criterion—the need for discrete details—is the most commonly utilized. One must demonstrate why the proposed source tradition is more probable than another. Many societies have analogous stories and traditions; for the parallel to be more than merely illustrative there must be discrete, distinct details betraying the original source. These could be linguistic terms or names, but could theoretically be anything. The difficulty of understanding the theory and transmission of myth should be cautionary here.[27] The last criterion, six, relates to the overall structure of the receiving tradition as it can be reconstructed. This is perhaps the vaguest and most difficult of the criteria to be demonstrated adequately, but it is necessary for the attempt to be made. As both Vroom and Light note, the introduction of new elements into a system often necessitates either a reinterpretation or a reorganization of other elements in the receiving tradition (as well as the reinterpretation of the element itself). Thus, a polytheistic religion that adopts a new god will most likely correspondingly modify the functions of other, similar gods in the pantheon, perhaps even replacing some of them. It is within this criterion that Light's discussion of symbols, categories, and organizational rules becomes most helpful. Each tradition has symbols and categories that are more central and others that are more peripheral. Central elements will be more resistant to influence, while more peripheral ones will be less so. When analyzing the structure of a proposed receiving tradition, it is necessary to determine the radicalness of the proposed element within the perspective of that tradition: the "organizational rules" of the receiving tradition must be taken into account. For example, the structural importance of monotheism in Christianity would lead one to expect that either no foreign deities would be adopted or would be adopted in a drastically different understanding to their original function. This, of course, fits the assimilation of deities as saints and angels: open categories in the Christian tradition in a way the category "divinity" is not. This is not the case in traditions such as Buddhism.[28]

---

27. For a concise explication, see Bowie, *Anthropology of Religion*, 267–304; cf. Caspo, *Theories of Mythology*.

28. Cf. Grayson, "Accommodation of Korean Folk Religion to the Religious Forms of Buddhism."

CONCLUSIONS

When seeking to understand the potential relevance of foreign traditions on the development of Second Temple Judaism and its texts, then, it is important to remember the types of interaction which could occur (not only quotations or direct, discrete borrowings, but influence, conscious and unconscious, positive and negative), as well as to consider the six different aspects related to the criteria noted above. Prior to analysis of particular texts or elements, however, must come at least a preliminary investigation of the structure of the two traditions in focus. The scholar must consider how the proposed interaction would have been perceived by contemporary Judaeans, who most likely had different priorities and perspectives than the contemporary scholar. Finally, the overall interpretive import must be considered. For a proposed instance of borrowing to be called "influence," to be convincing, and to relate more adequately to the ways real people function within living traditions, this combination of comparative structures and interpretive change is the most important aspect for analysis, although it is too often neglected. This principle is true whether the interaction was primarily through oral or textual media.[29]

---

29. A lengthy discussion of the relevance of Oral Theory to studies of inter-cultural and inter-religious influence is being pursued by the author elsewhere. In the meantime, the reader is directed to the valuable study of Niditch, *Oral World and Written Word*.

BIBLIOGRAPHY

Barr, James. "The Question of Religious Influence: The Case of Zoroastrianism, Judaism, and Christianity." *Journal of the American Academy of Religion* 53 (1985) 201–35.

Bowie, Fiona. *The Anthropology of Religion*. 2nd ed. Oxford: Blackwell, 2006.

Boyd, Robert, and Peter J. Richerson. *The Origin and Evolution of Cultures*. Oxford: Oxford University Press, 2005.

Caspo, Eric. *Theories of Mythology*. Ancient Cultures. Oxford: Blackwell, 2005.

Clarke, Joanne, editor. *Archaeological Perspectives on the Transmission and Transformation of Culture in the Eastern Mediterranean*. Levant Supplementary Series 2. Oxford: Oxbow, 2005.

Dallmayr, Fred. *Beyond Orientalism: Essays in Cross-Cultural Encounters*. Albany: SUNY Press, 1996.

Durham, William H. "Applications of Evolutionary Culture Theory." *Annual Review of Anthropology* 21 (1992) 331–55.

Goodenough, Ward H. "Phylogenetically Related Cultural Traditions." *Cross-Cultural Research* 31 (1997) 16–26.

Grayson, James H. "The Accommodation of Korean Folk Religion to the Religious Forms of Buddhism: An Example of Reverse Syncretism." *Asian Folklore Studies* 51 (1992) 199–217.

Hinnells, John R. "Zoroastrian Influence on the Judeo-Christian Tradition." *Journal of the K. R. Cama Oriental Institute* 45 (1976) 1–23.

Kraeling, Carl H. "Method in the Study of Religious Syncretism." *Journal of Bible and Religion* 9.1 (1941) 28–34, 66.

Lesser, Alexander. "Social Fields and the Evolution of Society." *Southwestern Journal of Anthropology* 17 (1961) 40–48.

Light, Timothy. "Orthosyncretism: An Account of Melding in Religion." *Method and Theory in the Study of Religion* 12 (2000) 162–185.

Niditch, Susan. *Oral World and Written Word: Ancient Israelite Literature*. Library of Ancient Israel. Louisville: Westminster John Knox, 1996.

Poole, Fitz John Porter. "Metaphors and Maps: Towards Comparison in the Anthropology of Religion." *Journal of the American Academy of Religion* 54 (1986) 411–57.

Sandmel, Samuel. "Parallelomania." *Journal of Biblical Literature* 81 (1962) 1–13.

Schultz, Richard L. *The Search for Quotation: Verbal Parallels in the Prophets*. JSOTSS 180. Sheffield: Sheffield Academic Press, 1999.

Shaked, Shaul. "Iranian Influence on Judaism: First Century B.C.E. to Second Century C.E." In *The Cambridge History of Judaism*. Vol. I: *Introduction; The Persian Period*, edited by W. D. Davies and L. Finkelstein, 308–25. Cambridge: Cambridge University Press, 2000.

Swadesh, Morris. "Diffusional Cumulation and Archaic Residue as Historical Explanations." *Southwestern Journal of Anthropology* 7 (1951) 1–21.

Talmon, Shemaryahu. "The 'Comparative Method' in Biblical Interpretation: Principles and Problems." In *Congress Volume: Göttingen, 1977*, 320–56. Vetus Testamentum Supplement 29. Leiden: Brill, 1978.

Vroom, Hendrik M. "Syncretism and Dialogue: a Philosophical Analysis." In *Syncretism in Religion: A Reader*, edited by Anita M. Leopold and Jeppe S. Jensen, 103–12. Critical Categories in the Study of Religion. London: Equinox, 2004.

Wold, Benjamin G. *Women, Men, and Angels: The Qumran Wisdom Document Musar leMevin and Its Allusions to Genesis Creation Traditions*. Wissenschaftliche Untersuchungen zum Neuen Testament 2/201. Tübingen: Mohr/Siebeck, 2005.

Wood, Irving P. "Borrowing between Religions." *Journal of Biblical Literature* 46 (1927) 98–105.

2

The Synagogue at Herodium
Problematic Fact or Problematic Fiction?

Lidia D. Matassa

INTRODUCTION

Herodium is an archaeological site at which a first-century synagogue was identified. The identification is generally accepted in the scholarship, but when we look at the archaeological and epigraphical evidence, it is revealed to be surprisingly flawed.

The archaeology of Herodium is such that destruction layers from both Jewish rebellions against Rome are mixed together.[1] Indeed, there is only one space in the immediate area where the synagogue was identified which could be identified as belonging only to the period of the first rebellion. This paper addresses the issue of how the synagogue identification was made using the excavation reports as well as the epigraphical and source material relating thereto, and I argue it has a flawed basis.

Herodium (consisting of an upper fortress and a lower palatial area) is located 12 km south of Jerusalem, just below the hills of Bethlehem (see Figure 2 below).

---

1. The first Jewish rebellion: 66–73 CE; second Jewish rebellion (the Bar-Kokhba rebellion): 132–135 CE.

FIGURE 2: Herodium (looking south from Bethlehem)

Virgilio Corbo, who excavated Herodium, uncovered a Roman triclinium in the upper fortress of Herodium, which he said may have been adapted for use as a synagogue. He ascribed the structure as belonging to the period of the "Jewish Wars," deliberately avoiding any specific chronological ascription. By the time the final excavation reports were published, however, Corbo had found sufficient archaeological evidence to be able to say that *if* the triclinium had been adapted for use as a synagogue, then this usage belonged to the period of the second rebellion. Others have since then argued that the changes to the triclinium belonged to the period of the first Jewish rebellion, and use this re-dating to support the synagogue identification; it is this argument which is generally accepted in the scholarship.

There is a fundamental disconnect between the two arguments, primarily because those who have ascribed the changes to the triclinium as belonging to the period of the first Jewish rebellion have simply ignored Corbo's findings.

There is a paucity of primary material, both textual and archaeological, relating to Herodium for the period of the first Jewish rebellion. Josephus, our only comprehensive source, deals with the construction of Herodium by Herod the Great, but barely mentions it in the context of the rebellion.

JOSEPHUS'S HERODIUM NARRATIVE

Josephus tells us that Herodium was built on the spot where Herod, when retreating from Jerusalem to Masada in flight from Antigonus and the massed Parthian armies in 40 BCE, achieved one of his most important victories over the Hasmonaeans and their allies. Herodium was built some time between 24 BCE and 15 BCE (*Ant* 14.359–60; *JW* 1.265), and consists of a lower palace with gardens and swimming pools, and an upper palace-fortress. This layout, according to Josephus, gave Lower Herodium the appearance of a town, and Upper Herodium the appearance of a castle stronghold (*Ant* 15.323–25; 17.196–99; *JW* 1.419; 1.670–73; 3.55).

Josephus said that Herod furnished both the upper and lower parts lavishly and brought in an abundant water supply to an area which was generally arid. He says that the upper site was adorned with round towers and that there was a route to the summit via two hundred steps of pure white marble (*Ant* 15.323–25; 16.13, 17.196–99; *JW* 1.419; 1.670–73; 3.55).

In addition to building Lower and Upper Herodium, Herod also designed Herodium as the site of his mausoleum, and Josephus tells us of the lavish funeral procession culminating in his burial (*Ant* 17.199; *JW* 1.670–73).[2] The account of the funeral procession is the last mention of Herodium by Josephus until he begins his account of the Jewish rebellion against Rome in the late 60s CE.

Josephus tells us that during the Jewish rebellion, Herodium, Masada, and Machaerus were the last three rebel desert strongholds to hold out against Roman forces. In 71 CE, Herodium became the first of these three to fall to the Tenth Legion Fretensis, then under the command of Lucilius Bassus (*JW* 4.554–55).

Given the foregoing, we might expect that Josephus would have then spent some time describing what happened at Herodium during the first Jewish rebellion, but he barely touches on it. It does not seem to have posed much of a threat to the Romans and was captured by them *en route* to Machaerus (*JW* 7.163).

Josephus does not give us any detail relating to the fall of Herodium to the Romans. For Herodium during the first Jewish rebellion, there was to be no narrative relating heroic deeds by brave defenders, no motif of

---

2. Ehud Netzer of the Hebrew University of Jerusalem recently discovered what he has identified as Herod's tomb on the southeastern side of the hill of Upper Herodium.

mass-suicide, no account of the final desperate hours before the fall, and no mention of survivors or deaths on either side.

THE PALACE-FORTRESS OF HERODIUM

Herod went to extraordinary lengths—even by his standards—to construct Upper Herodium, first creating an artificial hill on which to locate it, and then building the fortress on the hill, raising it well above the local landscape (see Figure 2 above). The circular upper Palace-fortress is surrounded by a casement wall with four towers protruding from it (see Figure 3 below).

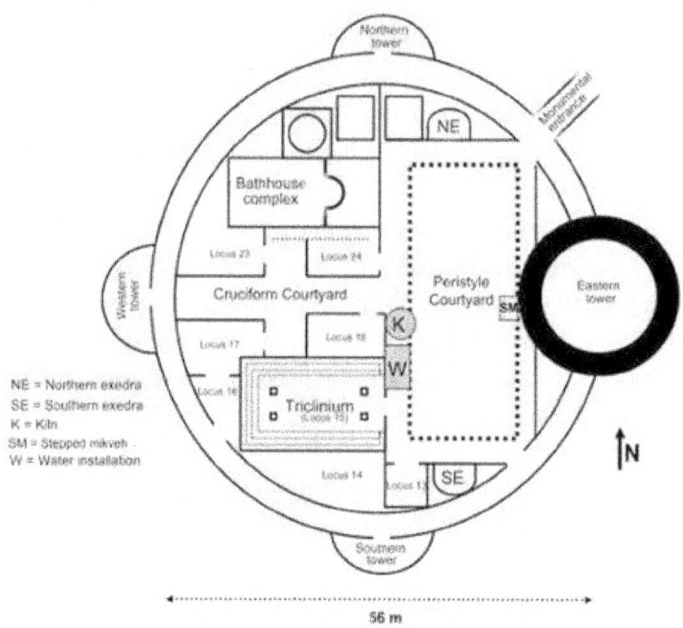

FIGURE 3: Context and Locations

The outer diameter of the casement wall is 63m and the inner diameter of the palace-fortress is 56m. The casement is made up of two parallel walls 3.4m apart, forming a circular corridor around the footprint of Upper Herodium. When it was built, this structure extended some 25m above the artificial hill and was divided into—possibly—as many as seven stories, including two underground cellar/cistern levels. The upper storeys had ceilings and floors supported on wooden beams and were each encircled by the casement corridor/rooms, which probably served for habitation, storerooms and access.³

Four towers protrude out from the casement wall; three semicircular ones (on the south, west and north) and one circular one on the east (see Figure 3 above). The circular tower extends inside the fortress as well as out.⁴

Access to the palace-fortress was from the northeast, via a stairway that Josephus described as having 200 stone steps of white marble (*JW* 1.419).⁵ When the construction work was completed, earth and gravel was piled up around it, creating steep slopes and giving the hill its iconic conical volcanic shape (see Figure 2 above).⁶

Internally, the fortress is divided into two main sections. The structure with which this chapter is concerned—the triclinium identified as a synagogue—is located in the western section (see Figure 3 above). The western section contains the triclinium, various ancillary rooms and a bathhouse complex. A cross-shaped courtyard separates the triclinium and ancillary rooms from the bathhouse complex just 30m to the north of the triclinium. The eastern section of the palace-fortress is taken up by a large peristyle courtyard.⁷

THE EXCAVATIONS

Between 1962 and 1967 Virgilio Corbo conducted excavations at the site on behalf of the Studium Biblicum Franciscanum, during which time the main buildings on the summit were uncovered and mapped. He identified the triclinium in the upper palace-fortress as a synagogue, initially attributing it to the period of the "Jewish Wars."⁸

Between 1967 and 1970, Gideon Foerster of the Hebrew University of Jerusalem carried out preservation and restoration works for the National Parks Authority. During these works, a network of cisterns and an system of tunnels dug in the hill that dated to the time of the Bar-Kokhba revolt were uncovered.⁹ In 1970, Ehud Netzer excavated sections of Lower

3. Netzer, *Architecture of Herod*, 183.
4. Corbo, "L'Herodion de Giabel Fureidis," 74.
5. Netzer, *Architecture of Herod*, 187.
6. Ibid., 188.
7. Netzer, "Herodium," 619.
8. Corbo, "L'Herodion," 103.
9. Netzer, "Herodium," 618.

Herodium.¹⁰ Netzer is currently involved in the ongoing excavation of what he has identified as Herod's tomb, as well as in preservation works on Upper Herodium.¹¹

THE IDENTIFICATION OF THE TRICLINIUM AS A SYNAGOGUE

In his preliminary report published in 1967, Virgilio Corbo, the original excavator of Upper Herodium, identified the triclinium as a synagogue. He said that the triclinium was occupied and transformed during the period of the "Jewish Wars" ("le guerre giudache") and that it was the construction of benches around its walls that identified it as a synagogue.¹²

Outside the northeastern wall of the triclinium he found a three-pool water installation which he identified as a mikveh, as well as a large kiln (see Figure 4 below).¹³

In the final excavation reports published in 1989, Corbo went further than in his preliminary reports, and categorized the converted triclinium as belonging to the period of the second Jewish rebellion (132–135 CE).¹⁴ Corbo's identification of the synagogue as belonging to the second rebellion period has given subsequent scholars something of a headache, and, indeed, most of those who have written about the triclinium/synagogue have simply ignored Corbo's reports, saying that the use of the triclinium as a synagogue dates to the period of the first rebellion. However, as is discussed below, there is little evidence to substantiate that claim.

The Excavation Reports

Corbo's identification of the space as a synagogue is based on the fact that the room has benches around three walls and, presumably, because it was occupied by Jews.¹⁵ It is worth noting here that Corbo made his identification in 1967, and Yigael Yadin had identified a synagogue on Masada in 1965.¹⁶

10. Ibid.
11. http://www.haaretz.com/hasen/spages/856808.html.
12. Corbo, "L'Herodion," 103.
13. Corbo, *Herodion*, vol. 1, 74–75.
14. Ibid., 74–75.
15. Corbo, "L'Herodion," 102.
16. Netzer, "Masada," 974.

The Converted Triclinium

Corbo described the Herodian period triclinium as a large rectangular room measuring 15.15m x 10.60m, with an entrance overlooking the peristyle courtyard to the east. There were a number of rooms around the triclinium, but only two of these were connected with it (Loci 14 and 18—see Figure 4 below). Corbo said that these two loci were not related to its usage as a synagogue, since the northern and southern access doorways from the triclinium to those rooms had been bricked-up when the triclinium was converted. There were two windows on the eastern façade that had also been bricked up when the triclinium was converted.[17]

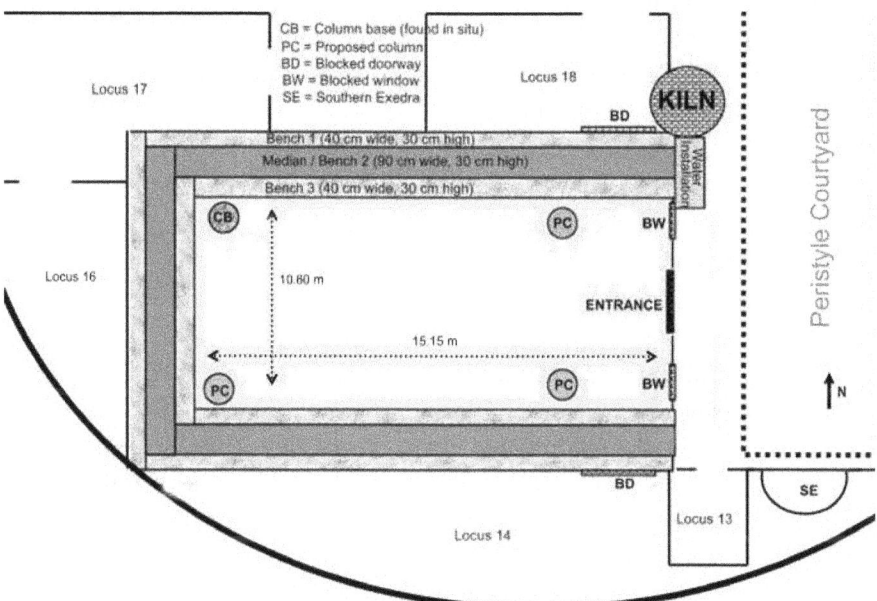

FIGURE 4: The Triclinium

The area of the triclinium was the single largest space excavated in Upper Herodium. During the Herodian phase, according to Corbo, it had a wooden roof supported by four columns, although only one column base was found *in situ* (see Figure 4 above).[18]

The conversion of the triclinium into a synagogue, according to Corbo, involved the construction of benches around the walls and the

17. Corbo, "L'Herodion," 101.
18. Ibid.

blocking off of the northern and southern doors and the two windows on the eastern façade. The entrance on the eastern façade was also made narrower at this time.[19] Three benches/steps were added in the triclinium, and these were built of stone blocks taken from the walls of the triclinium as well as some reused architectural pieces from elsewhere on Upper Herodium.

The top bench is 40cm wide and 30cm high, the middle bench (or median) is 90cm wide and 30cm high, and the bottom bench is 40cm wide and 30cm high. The benches/steps run from the jamb of the blocked door on the north wall, around the western wall and almost to the jamb of the blocked door on the southern wall (see Figure 4 above). Corbo could not determine whether the steps/benches broke off at the northern and southern doors intentionally, or whether this was due to subsequent destruction.[20] Corbo said that pieces of capitals built into the benches around the north, south and western walls may have come from the columns that originally supported the roof. He said the structural changes (the blocking up of the windows and doors and the construction of the benches) signalled the change of usage from triclinium to synagogue.[21]

By the northeastern façade of the triclinium, Corbo uncovered what he described as a three-pooled mikveh.[22] Abutting the northern edge of this installation is a large kiln (see Figure 4 above).[23] Corbo does not discuss why a mikveh and a kiln might be located together in this way. I shall discuss this below.

By the time he published the final excavation reports (the first volume was published in 1989), Corbo had come to the conclusion that the structural changes in the triclinium, which he said had transformed it into a synagogue, had to be attributed to the period of the second Jewish rebellion.[24] The basis on which Corbo came to this conclusion was very

19. Ibid., 102.
20. Ibid., 103.
21. Ibid., 102.

22. The water installation was completely buried beneath the sand in the years after the Corbo excavations. From 1999 through to my most recent visit to the site in February 2009, only the kiln remained visible. However, since then conservation work being undertaken by the Hebrew University of Jerusalem has uncovered the water installation again.

23. Corbo, *Herodion*, 75.
24. Ibid.

simply that that the material evidence pointed to the period of the second rebellion and that very little evidence remained *at all* that pointed to an earlier period. In fact, the *only* evidence—other than coins—that Corbo could safely attribute to the period of the first revolt were some wooden plates found in context with some first rebel period coins. The wooden plates and coins were found in Locus 17, which had no connection with the triclinium itself. Its access was via the cruciform courtyard (see Figure 4 above).[25]

According to Corbo, the Herodian period floor of Locus 17 had been completely destroyed and was about one metre lower than the floor of the first rebel period. On the rebel period floor, sixteen coins were found (nine of year 2 of the rebellion, one of year 3, and six which were too worn to date).[26] Wooden plates were also found in this context.[27] Also found were a Corinthian capital, a section of hypocaust from the bathhouse and a large ballista.[28]

Locus 18 borders the triclinium and the cruciform courtyard (see Figure 4 above). Originally, there was a connection between this Locus 18 and the triclinium. The original doorway between the north wall of the triclinium and Locus 18 mirrors the doorway between the south wall of the triclinium and Locus 14. However, both of these doors were blocked up during the conversion of the triclinium.[29]

Locus 13 is the room to the south of the peristyle courtyard, in front of the southern tower. It measures 4.21m x 4.10m and to its east is the southern exedra (see Figure 4 above). Its entrance was via the peristyle courtyard. It was occupied during the period of the second rebellion and when it was excavated was buried beneath a debris layer almost 2m deep. Amongst the debris of this layer was one coin from the second rebellion (which was too worn to be dated).[30] In the area between Locus 13 and the wall of the triclinium, a hoard of 770 second rebellion period coins and some scattered coins of the same period were excavated.[31]

---

25. Corbo, "L'Herodion," 107.
26. A. Spijkerman, *Herodion III*, 21.
27. Corbo, "L'Herodion," 107.
28. Ibid.
29. Ibid., 109.
30. Spijkerman, *Herodion III*, 17–21.
31. Ibid., 23–83.

The importance of the level around this area was derived, according to Corbo, from the fact that it dated to the period of the second rebellion and the deep destruction layer indicated the intensity the rebel defence of Herodium against the Romans in 135 CE.[32]

Discussion

The only explanation I can find for Corbo's identification of a synagogue in Upper Herodium in 1967 is that it was influenced by Yigael Yadin's identification of what he claimed was a synagogue at Masada only two years earlier. Indeed, Corbo mentioned Yigael Yadin's synagogue identification (which was widely publicised and achieved iconic status).[33]

Without reference to the Yadin identification, all there is at Herodium is a converted triclinium with stepped benches around three of the walls, two blocked up doors, two blocked up windows and a nearby mikveh (not the one identified by Corbo, but another one on the other side of the peristyle courtyard, beside the eastern tower), nor was any material found inside or near the triclinium which might indicate its use.

Corbo's identification of a synagogue has been widely accepted by scholars, although those who have written about it have ascribed it to the period of the first Jewish rebellion, even though no material was found in the triclinium or even in any of the rooms which had previously been connected to it (Loci 14 and 18). The only locus in which material was discovered in a context which could be clearly identified as belonging to the first Jewish rebellion was Locus 17, which was not connected to the triclinium (see Figure 3 above).

Since most of the material discovered in this area (and elsewhere in Upper Herodium) belongs to the period of the second rebellion, Corbo assumed that the amendments to the triclinium were contemporary with that period. Of course, it is possible that the benches were put in place earlier, but there is no evidence to support this.

Abutting the triclinium is what Corbo described as a mikveh. This structure itself is beside a large second rebellion period kiln. The water installation is a three-pool system, so that if it were a mikveh, one might have had to enter one pool, exit it, enter the next, exit that and then enter

---

32. Corbo, "L'Herodion," 76.
33. Corbo, *Herodion*, 75.

and exit the final pool and is, I think, unlikely to be connected to any sort of religious ritual.

Moreover, the size of the adjoining kiln (with a diameter of 2m) suggests it could have been used on an industrial scale, and I would suggest that the three pools, rather than being a mikveh, relate directly to the kiln and were perhaps used for the purpose of processing clay and firing pottery, or for some other manufacturing process. Unfortunately, at the time of the excavations, no tests were conducted on either the water installation or the kiln that could have indicated the purposes for which they were used.[34]

Other than this *sort* of explanation, the association of a kiln and a water installation just does not make sense. The heat of the kiln would cause the water in a mikveh to evaporate (since both stones and bricks conduct heat), making it difficult to maintain the volume of water required for ritual purification purposes and perhaps even making it uncomfortable to use. There is no reason to have a three-pooled structure for ritual purification when all that is required is ritual immersion—not facilities for bathing. Furthermore, there *is* a mikveh on the other side of the peristyle courtyard, just 25m away, and it is a simple stepped pool into which a person could step, immerse and exit quickly and easily (see Figure 5 below). If the triclinium *was* a synagogue, and if it *were* established that synagogues were found in association with mikva'ot, then the stepped mikveh on the far side of the peristyle courtyard would be the one related to the triclinium.

---

34. Corbo, *Herodion*, 75.

24 A LAND LIKE YOUR OWN

FIGURE 5: Mikveh, Triclinium, Kiln, and Water Installation

The mikveh shown above at Figure 5 is a second rebellion period structure, constructed out of the same sorts of material used in converting the triclinium.[35] This, while not being conclusive evidence, lends some weight to Corbo's identification of the structural changes in the triclinium as belonging to the second rebellion period.[36]

During the period of the second rebellion, the occupants of the fortress made minor structural changes to most of the buildings to suit their needs. Evidence of their work was found in the area of the peristyle courtyard on the east and in the bathhouse and the triclinium on the west. Ovens for domestic use were also found, as well as the aforementioned kiln and associated water installation. All of these installations contained material from the second rebellion period only.[37]

---

35. Corbo, "L'Herodion," 76.
36. Ibid.
37. Ibid.

THE COINS FROM THE FORTRESS

Over the four seasons of excavations on Herodium between 1962 and 1967, a total of 873 coins were found. The majority of these coins belonged to the period of the Bar Kokhba revolt. Of these, 770 were found in a single horde in the space between Locus 13 and the triclinium (see Figure 3 above). A further sixteen coins were found in rooms elsewhere in the palace-fortress, giving a total of 786 second rebellion period coins. Another forty coins of miscellaneous dates (belonging neither to the first nor second rebellions) were found. These included coins from the second century BCE though the seventh century CE.[38]

Only 47 coins relating to the period of the first revolt were found, and these were found scattered in various rooms around the fortress. Of these forty-seven coins, twenty-seven were from year two of the rebellion, twelve from year three, two were undated and six were too faded and/or damaged and/or worn to be read.[39]

The coins can tell us a little about the period of the first rebellion. They tell us that Herodium may have been occupied from at least the second year of the rebellion (67–68 CE) and that this occupation may have lasted until at least the third year (68–69 CE). Of course, none of this is certain. It is possible that the first rebel period coins may have been in the hands of the rebels during the second rebellion. Coins of bronze, silver and gold retained the value of the metal they were made of and would not have gone out of use, unless they were melted down to make something else.

INSCRIPTIONS AND OSTRACA

There was little written material found at Herodium, and certainly nothing that would indicate a system of organization of the occupants during the second rebellion period. In fact, most of the written material found on Herodium was merely graffiti scratched on the plaster of the bathhouse walls, various ostraca and writing on jars.[40]

The ostraca and jar inscriptions, which were written in Greek, Aramaic, and Hebrew, belong to the main periods of settlement; that is, to the Herodian and/or to the first and second Jewish rebellions. On the ba-

---

38. Spijkerman, *Herodion III*, 17–21.
39. Ibid.
40. There were only around 100 ostraca found in all at Herodium.

sis of this material, Corbo said it was impossible to differentiate between inscriptions from the time of Herod and from the two revolts.⁴¹

However, some of the material could be safely attributed to the second century CE. An *abecedary* was found in the kiln adjacent to the triclinium, containing two complete Hebrew alphabets on one side and an incomplete alphabet (up to the letter ס) on the other. At nearby Wadi el-Murabba'at, nine similar *abecedary* dating to the second century CE were found.⁴² The presence of an *abecedary* does suggest that some sort of teaching or scribal activity was taking place here during the second century, certainly in the period of the Bar-Kokhba rebellion.⁴³

A small ostracon was found in the kiln abutting the triclinium. In the excavation reports of 1972, Emmanuelle Testa translated the text of this ostracon—גדול ספח סבי דגון—as "Dagon my ancestor is among the nobility."⁴⁴ The verb ספח means "to grow, or to swell, or to add to," or possibly "to spontaneously regrow." Dagon is the name of the Philistine deity, and since the kiln and the water installation are associated together, it is difficult to understand how this might relate to a religious Jewish context.

Another ostracon was found in the water installation on which was inscribed two words in Aramaic lettering. These two words are גלא תן, which Testa tentatively translated as "instructs the exiles" or, possibly, "repeat again the exile."⁴⁵ the word גלא can also be translated as a "heap" (i.e., of stones or bones), or "to be uncovered," or to "go into exile." This text could therefore be translated as "give [a] heap [of something]," or "give [into] exile."

Another inscription, written on the belly of a large jar, was found in the water installation. This inscription comprised two words in Aramaic script. The words are רבא ירסא, which Testa suggested could translate as "poison the high power."⁴⁶

---

41. Testa, *Herodion IV*, 93.
42. Ibid., 77–78.
43. Ibid., 107.
44. Ibid., 80.
45. Ibid., 81.
46. Ibid., 82.

The term ירסא רבא is not found in biblical texts. It is, however, cited in Jastrow's dictionary of the Mishnah.[47] Testa's translation of these words as "poison the high power" is an interesting possibility, but is it a likely one? It is true that ריס is found in Jastrow meaning "a drop," or "poison," but Testa has coupled it in this form with רבא as a noun and used "poison" as a verb, translating it as "poison the high power." Jastrow says that the word appears in the same form in the Targum to Psalm 58:5 and is identical to ארס, "poison." Therefore, if ירסא were a noun, then "great poison" *could* be the meaning. This text might have been attached to goods or merchandise that was poisonou, which makes more sense on a large jar then Testa's unusual translation. Ultimately, however, the meaning remains uncertain.[48]

Discussion

None of the ostraca (or jar inscriptions) from Herodium speak to the existence of, or the necessity for, a synagogue during the period of the first or second rebellions. And, unlike at Masada (where the ostraca numbered over 800 and attested to the existence of an administrative system of some complexity), there were only a hundred or so ostraca found on Herodium. Against this, however, the *abecedaries* suggest that there was some form of organized administration going on at Herodium during the second century revolt and, perhaps, that this was taking place in the assembly space into which the triclinium had been converted.

THE LITERARY EVIDENCE

Most references to Herodium prior to the second Jewish rebellion relate to its construction during the reign of Herod the Great, to its location, and to Herod's burial there. Material relating to the occupation of Herodium during the first Jewish rebellion is sparse and what we do know comes to us in its entirety from Josephus. Unlike his descriptions of the fortress at Masada, Josephus does not give any details of numbers, time-span, alterations, or even details of the siege and eventual taking of Herodium by the Romans.

> When Cerealis had conquered them he went to Hebron, another very ancient city. I have told you already, that this city is situated in a mountainous country not far off Jerusalem; and when

---

47. Jastrow, *Dictionary*, 597, 124.
48. In discussion with Prof. Catherine Hezser, Head of Jewish Studies at SOAS.

> he had broken into the city by force what multitude and young men were left therein he slew and burnt down the city; so that as now all the places were taken, excepting Herodium and Masada, and Machaerus, which were in possession of the robbers, so Jerusalem was what the Romans at present aimed at. (Josephus *JW* 4.554–55)[49]

In the foregoing passage we are told only that the strongholds of Masada, Herodium, and Machaerus were still in the hands of the rebels. The Roman strategy was to deal with the rebellious cities such as Hebron and Jerusalem before concerning themselves with ridding themselves of the rebels at Masada, Herodium, and Machaerus.

> Meanwhile, Lucilius Bassus had been dispatched to Judæa as legate, and, taking over the command from Cerealis Vetilianus, had reduced the fortress of Herodium with its garrison to surrender. He next concentrated all the numerous scattered detachments of troops, including the tenth legion, having determined to march against Machaerus. This fortress it was absolutely necessary to eradicate, lest its strength should induce many to revolt; since the nature of the place was specially adapted to inspire its occupants with high hopes of security and to deter and alarm its assailants. (Josephus *JW* 7.163)

In this second passage, it would appear that Herodium did not pose any great military difficulty to the Romans. The implication is that the scattered troops referred to by Josephus were not deemed necessary to besiege Herodium and, perhaps, that only troops immediately available were sent. Josephus does not describe the capture of Herodium but instead discusses the strategic importance of Machaerus. One might expect, if the rebels at Herodium had posed a threat to the Romans, that Josephus would have included some detail as to its defensive systems, the people there, etc., as he had done with Masada.

> The Zealots, in consequence, alarmed at his designs and anxious to forestall one who growing strength was to their injury, went out with their main body under arms; Simon met them and in the ensuing fight killed many of them and drove the remainder into the city. Misgivings about his forces, however, still deterred him from an assault on the walls; instead he resolved first to subdue Idumaea, and now marched with an army of twenty thousand men

---

49. Translations follow the Loeb editions.

towards the frontiers of that country. The chieftains of Idumaea hastily mustered from the country their most efficient troops, numbering about twenty-five thousand, and leaving the mass of the population to protect their property against incursions of the *Sicarii* of Masada, met Simon at the frontier. There he fought them and, after a battle lasting all day, left the field neither victor nor vanquished; he then withdrew to Nain and the Idumaeans disbanded to their homes. Not long after, however, Simon [bar Gioras] with a yet larger force again invaded their territory, and, encamping at a village called Tekoa, sent one of his comrades named Eleazar to the garrison at Herodion, which was not far off, to persuade them to hand over that fortress. The guards, ignorant of the subject of his visit, promptly admitted him, but at the first mention of the word "surrender" drew their swords and pursued him, until, finding escape impossible, he flung himself from the ramparts into the valley below and was killed on the spot. (Josephus *JW* 4.514–20)

This passage at least gives us some information about the group of rebels in control of Herodium, still, we do not know whether they occupied Herodium during the entire period of the first rebellion. We do not know when they arrived there, whether they had to wrest control of it from the Romans through force or treachery (as at Masada, *JW* 2.408) or whether it was unoccupied and their taking of it was unopposed. We do not know what condition Herodium was in when it was occupied during the period of the first rebellion. Nor do we have any idea of the number of rebels there, or how they were organized. We know only that (possibly) Zealot or Idumaean factions of rebels occupied and had control of Herodium, although we do not know how long for, or who comprised those groups of people.

Discussion

These three references represent the totality of material from Josephus relating to Herodium during the period of the first rebellion. They are clearly of no assistance in any discussion of a synagogue identification, nor are they of great assistance in identifying who exactly occupied Herodium, nor for how long.

THE SCHOLARSHIP

The scholarship on the subject of Herodium follows the same pattern as the scholarship on Masada, Gamla, Jericho, and Delos. That is, an archaeologist (usually the excavator) declares that the building is a synagogue, and thereafter practically every scholar repeats the claim, often with variations and embellishment. This pattern of repetition reinforces errors made in the process of identifying synagogues belonging to the pre-70 CE period.

I should point out that as with Masada, the excavators, including Corbo, have referred throughout their reports to the rebels as "Zealots," although Josephus never identifies any of the occupants of Herodium specifically as Zealots. Describing the rebel occupants of Herodium (and elsewhere) as Zealots clearly sets up a scenario where there *could* be reason to establish a synagogue, even if there is no other evidence to support that identification. If the rebels are identified as brigands, Sicarii, mercenaries, political rebels, etc., then the identification of religious buildings becomes far more problematic.

Gideon Foerster (1981)

Foerster performed conservation work at Upper Herodium after the Corbo excavations had ceased. He describes the physical layout of the triclinium, attributing the post-Herodian structural changes as belonging to the period of the first Jewish rebellion, particularly the benches, which were built of architectural fragments taken from other areas of Herod's palace.[50]

He goes on to compare the Herodium triclinium with the building identified as a synagogue on Masada, saying that their layout is "essentially identical." He attributes this similarity to "Zealot construction" on the site. He says that in neither Masada nor Herodium has a fixed Torah shrine been found, although at Masada a side room may have functioned as a repository, since scroll fragments were discovered there. He goes on to say that at Herodium, one of the smaller rooms flanking the hall may have served this purpose.[51] He also notes that in the cases of both Herodium

---

50. Foerster, "Synagogues at Masada and Herodium," 24.
51. Ibid., 26.

and Masada there is a nearby mikveh and that at Herodium, the mikveh actually abutted the eastern wall of the synagogue.[52]

Foerster argues that the two structures identified as synagogues on Masada and Herodium are almost identical in dimensions: Masada 12m x 15m; Herodium 10.5m x 15m, and that they were undoubtedly constructed along with the other structures at these sites, although significant modifications were made in both of them during the First Revolt against Rome, when these buildings fell into the hands of the insurgents.[53]

Discussion

Foerster does not explain his reasons for rejecting Corbo's dating, other than saying that the triclinium's structural changes "most likely" occurred in the period of the first rebellion—on the basis of a comparison with the structure at Masada, which has also been identified as a belonging to the first rebellion period synagogue—and that the two structures are "essentially identical: oblong halls lined with benches and with supporting columns in the space of the hall proper."[54]

However, the identification of a synagogue at Masada is highly debatable (as I have argued elsewhere) and arguments for it are themselves based only on comparisons with—in essence, itself—and a structure at Gamla, also identified as a first-century synagogue.[55] This does not appear to me to be sufficient evidence to make such an identification at Herodium.

The structures at Masada and Gamla do share some features—the benches, the rectangular shape of the room, but that is as far as the similarities go. The triclinium at Herodium is in fact easily twice the size of Locus 1042 on Masada, although this does not bear on its identification. I neglected to take measurements when I visited the sites in 1999, 2004, 2005, 2006, and 2009, but the photographs I took *do* show the size difference between the two structures.

---

52. Ibid..
53. Ibid., 24.
54. Ibid.
55. Matassa, "On the Identification of Pre-70 C.E. Synagogues in the Land of Israel."

32 A LAND LIKE YOUR OWN

FIGURE 6: Comparison of Locus 1042 on Masada and the Triclinium at Herodium

Foerster has accepted the details of Corbo's excavation reports in relation to the triclinium on Herodium, but has attributed them to the period of the first rebellion on the basis of a superficial similarity with the building identified as a synagogue at Masada. This seems to me to be a inadequate reason to make the identification in terms of both time-line and structure. However, his short article, published in *Ancient Synagogues Revealed* in 1981, is the point at which the identification of the triclinium as a first-rebellion synagogue became well established and on which all subsequent scholarship has been based.

Joseph Patrich (1992)

In a review of Corbo's final excavation reports, Patrich says that "the synagogue" is better dated to the period of the first Jewish rebellion because of its resemblance to the structures at Masada and Gamla. He says that the majority of coins scattered about the site date from the First Jewish War. However, he then goes on to say that of the coins found on the site, 47 relate to the period of the first rebellion, and only 16 coins to the period of the second rebellion "if we disregard a hoard of approximately 1,000 bronze coins from this period found in the southern exedra."[56]

Patrich says that it is hard to understand why Corbo insisted on attributing most of the installations and alterations in the Herodian palace-fortress to the Second Revolt. He says that there is no plan in the final reports illustrating the state of the construction during the period of the first rebellion and that only in room 17 could Corbo define a stratigraphic distinction between the remains from the two revolts.[57]

He goes on to say that his conclusions are further supported because the Zealots at Masada went through significant efforts to build a synagogue and several mikva'ot. Thus, he claims, because a similar group inhabited Herodium during the period of the first Jewish rebellion, it seems likely that they would have followed suit. Moreover, since the fortress was in the possession of the rebels from about 66 to 71 CE, they certainly had ample time to make renovations to the triclinium.[58]

Discussion

Patrich disregards the lack of evidence relating to the period of the first rebellion, and imposes an unsupported conclusion based on a comparison and some assumptions. First, we do *not* know that Zealots occupied Herodium. Second, the reason there is no plan in Corbo's final excavation reports showing the construction phase relating to the period of the first rebellion *is that there were no built structures that could be so identified.* Corbo was quite clear on this point.[59]

56. Patrich, "Corbo's Excavations at Herodium," 243.

57. Ibid.

58. Ibid.

59. Corbo, *Herodion*, 69–70: "In our excavations, given the huge build up of the second Roman destruction, it is difficult to distinguish what belonged to the first destruction of the Herodian fortress. We could only safely differentiate wooden plates which were found associated with coins of the first revolt. Coins of the first revolt was also found between the peristyle and the north exedra, in the peristyle, and in the tower" (my translation).

The fact that 47 coins of the period of the first rebellion were found scattered around the site must be weighed against the discovery of the hoard of 770 coins of the period of the second rebellion being found (they were found between Locus 13 and the triclinium, not in the southern exedra as Patrich says).[60] Another sixteen second rebellion period coins were found in various rooms. Patrich has simply disregarded this evidence and has treated the first rebellion period coins as though they could *only* have been in use during the first rebellion. All in all, Patrich's contentions in his review are not supported by the evidence.

Ehud Netzer (1993)

Netzer reiterates Foerster's position, describing the architectural layout of the palace-fortress. He says that many archaeological traces of settlement were found from both the first and second revolts, and that settlement is also known from the literary sources. He says that the rebels' building activities were not extensive, being generally limited to the addition of walls in dry construction and the reuse of stones but that more basic changes—of a religious and cultic nature—were made in the triclinium, where rows of stone benches were added along three of the walls. Netzer says that this structure was apparently was used as a synagogue by the rebels who had taken refuge here and that a mikveh "appears to have been added when the building became a synagogue."[61]

Discussion

Netzer's contention that many archaeological traces of settlement changes were found relating to the period of the first rebellion is not supported by the excavation reports or any of the material evidence found on the site. Netzer links the water installation to the structural changes in the triclinium which, since they belong to the period of the second rebellion, does not support his argument. While Netzer has written extensively on the subject of Herod's building programme, he does not add anything new to the identification argument, merely repeating Foerster's contention that the structural changes in the triclinium belong to the period of the first rebellion.

60. Spijkerman, *Herodion III*, 23–83.
61. Netzer, "Herodium," 620.

Paul Flesher (1995)

Flesher takes a more cautious approach, and deals with the issue of the identification in general, saying of Masada, Herodium and Gamla that their Jewish character is evident only from their location within an area identified with Jews and that the architectural features that have been used to identify them as synagogues—the benches around the walls and the columns—appear also in structures not identified as synagogues, only some of which are Jewish.[62]

Flesher says that there is no way to identify what the triclinium was used for in the rebel period and that Herodium was the location of a rebel army which, like the rebels at Masada, needed a place to plan military strategy.[63]

Flesher goes on to say that there is also a chronological problem with the dating "of the synagogue" at Herodium, that the main proponent of this argument was Gideon Foerster who supervised the restoration of the site after the primary excavations had been completed and who argued that the synagogue dates to the first Jewish rebellion, although Corbo states that the synagogue belongs to the Bar Kokhba rebellion. Flesher concludes that the structure at Herodium provides "no sure evidence of a synagogue in the first century; if it is a synagogue, it most likely stems from the early second century."[64]

Donald Binder (1999)

Binder repeats Foerster's arguments in some detail and acknowledges that the synagogue identification was made on the basis of similarities with the structures on Masada and Gamla, and that Foerster and Netzer defended this proposal, which has since been adopted by many other archaeologists.[65]

Discussion

Binder reiterates Foerster's work, adding that the structures were "hewn out of the western side of the Herodian peristyle court by the rebels."[66]

---

62. Flesher, "Palestinian Synagogues Before 70 C.E.," 37.
63. Ibid.
64. Ibid., 37–38.
65. Binder, *Into the Temple Courts*, 184.
66. Ibid., 183.

While Binder acknowledges Corbo's attribution of the structural changes to the period of the second rebellion, he says that "nowhere in his report does Corbo defend his new position with arguments from archaeology."[67] In fact, Corbo based his conclusion on the material found in each archaeological context. Moreover, Binder can suggest no archaeological reason for Foerster's and Netzer's identification other than the superficial similarities between the structures at Masada, Herodium and Gamla.

Lee I. Levine (2005)

Levine takes a minimalist cautious position, merely pointing out the architectural layout of the triclinium. He does not undertake any analysis of the excavation reports or add any new information or analysis.[68]

Stephen Catto (2007)

Catto reiterates the same argument as Foerster, Netzer, Binder, and others, referring to the rebel occupants as "Zealots." He also attributes the structural changes to the period of the first rebellion. He says that Herodium offers little in the way of allowing a comfortable assertion that this room is a synagogue,[69] but that since it is capable of seating around 200 people, it was clearly used for communal purposes; the mikveh next to the building suggests that it was used for some ritual purpose, and the benches are "very similar to the ones found in other places which have been more confidently identified as synagogue buildings."[70]

Discussion

Catto's entire argument is based on Foerster's, Netzer's, and Binder's, and he does not add anything new, nor does he attempt to analyze the excavation reports for himself.

---

67. Ibid., 184.
68. Levine, *Ancient Synagogue*, 60.
69. Catto, *Reconstructing the First-Century Synagogue*, 93.
70. Ibid., 93.

CONCLUSIONS

Jewish rebels took control of Herodium some time after the beginning of the first rebellion against Rome.[71] It was eventually recaptured by the Romans before the fall of Masada and Machaerus. The site was then abandoned until the Bar Kokhba rebellion, when a group of rebels used it as an administrative and military base. In 135 CE, the Romans once more conquered Herodium and the site was again abandoned.

Given that the foregoing is all we actually know about Herodium, I find the identification there of a synagogue perplexing: there is just no evidence to support it. Even the debate about the dating of the structure is potentially irrelevant, as whatever period the triclinium related to there is still no evidence that it functioned as a synagogue (although, clearly, it *could* have been used as a synagogue).

Moreover, discussions about the architectural configuration of the room are irrelevant because beyond being a rectangular room with benches, there was nothing found in or near it to indicate it was used for religious purposes.

While material relating to the period of the first rebellion is lacking, there is specific reference to the period of the second rebellion found in Dio Cassius and in documents found at Wadi Murabba'at near Qumran. The Wadi Murabba'at documents say that Simeon Bar-Kokhba had a command post at Herodium.[72] Corbo cites two documents found at Wadi el-Murabba'at, both of which refer to land leases made "in Year Two of the liberation of Israel" and "by the authority of Simon bar Kokhba, Prince of Israel, who lives at Herodium."[73]

The documents found at Wadi el-Murabba'at suggest that there was a very settled community at Herodium during the period of the second rebellion, and that that community required administration. There is nothing, however, to suggest that this was the case for the occupation of Herodium during the period of the first rebellion. This may be because of the extent of the destruction of the site after the second rebellion, but there is unfortunately no way to know if this is the case.

---

71. Actually, there is nothing in the sources or the archaeological record to indicate whether they wrest it from Roman control or whether it lay abandoned before they occupied it.

72. Netzer, "Herodium," 618.

73. Corbo, *Herodion*, 70.

While Corbo initially struggled with the process of attributing structural changes in the buildings of the palace-fortress to either the first and/or second rebellion periods, by the time he wrote his final report he was convinced that most of the changes belonged to the period of the second rebellion. This seems relatively safe on the basis that there is a large second rebellion period kiln adjacent to the triclinium, and that there was a water installation associated with the kiln. We can perhaps surmise that whatever processes the kiln was used to facilitate, they required water either before or afterwards. The kiln is very large (2m in diameter), and it would seem logical to suggest that it was used for some industrial and/or military purpose, rather than for simple cooking or bread-making.

Corbo identified the triclinium as a synagogue on the basis of its similarity to a structure at Masada, but he attributed it and its structural changes (the addition of benches, the blocking up of the northern and southern doors and the two windows) to the period of the second rebellion on the basis that these changes were contemporary with the kiln and water installation.[74]

In general, it is likely that the changes to the triclinium were made at the same time as the development of the kiln and the associated water installation (which Corbo identified as a mikveh). The mikveh identification is problematic on the basis that the installation he describes is a three-pool complex in which one would first have to enter into a small pool, exit that pool, enter and exit a larger pool, and then enter and exit a third pool, all in a chamber directly connected to the large kiln. It seems improbable that a mikveh would be constructed in this manner, when it would be so easy to excavate a single pool with steps in the same space. Further, as I have already stated, there is a stepped mikveh just 20m away, across the peristyle courtyard, beside the eastern tower, which dates to the period of the second rebellion. It is constructed in the same manner as the benches in the triclinium, using reused blocks of stone and architectural fragments (see Figure 5 above).

The benches in the triclinium would have created a perfect space for a command and/or administrative centre and for a public meeting place to discuss issues in general with the population of Herodium. Thus, while the structure at Herodium is clearly an assembly hall, there is nothing to indicate that it was used for religious purposes. Since we know from the

---

74. Ibid., 75.

Wadi Murabba'at documents that the site was used as a command post by Simon bar Kokhba, the leader of the second rebellion, the assembly hall would be most reasonably attached to that time period because the rebels would have needed a place to assemble for military and strategic planning purposes.[75] It also appears, because of the discovery of the *abecedaries* in the kiln, that some sort of administrative/scribal/teaching function was going on in this place during the period of the second revolt.

Taking all of this into consideration and, in particular, the placement of a kiln and associated water installation beside the triclinium, the identification of this site as a synagogue is vexing and is difficult to explain . At best, if the triclinium was used as a synagogue, it was probably during the period of the second rebellion on the basis of the finds associated with that period.

75. Ibid., 37.

BIBLIOGRAPHY

Binder, Donald D. *Into the Temple Courts: The Place of the Synagogues in the Second Temple Period*. SBL Dissertation Series 169. Atlanta: Society of Biblical Literature, 1999

Cassius Dio. *Roman History*. Translated by Earnest Cary. Loeb Classical Library. London: Heinemann, 1925.

Catto, Stephen K. *Reconstructing the First-Century Synagogue*. Library of New Testament Studies 363. London: T. & T. Clark, 2007.

Chen, Doron. "The Design of the Ancient Synagogues in Judea: Masada and Herodium." *Bulletin of the American Schools of Oriental Research* 239 (1980) 37–40.

Corbo, Virgilio C. "The Excavation at Herodium." *Qadmoniot* 4 (1968) 132–36.

———. "Gébel Fureidis (Hérodium)." *Revue Biblique* 75 (1968) 424–28.

———. "L'Herodion de Giabel Fureidis." *Liber Annuus* 113 (1962–1963) 219–77.

———. "L'Herodion de Giabel Fureidis." *Liber Annuus* 117 (1967) 65–121.

———. *Herodion: Gli Edifici della Reggia-Fortrezza*. Vol. 1. Jerusalem: Franciscan Printing Press, 1989.

Flesher, Paul V. M. "Palestinian Synagogues Before 70 CE, a Review of the Evidence." In *Ancient Synagogues, Historical Analysis and Archaeological Discovery*, edited by Dan Urman and Paul V. M. Flesher, vol. 1, 27–39. Studia post-Biblica 47. Leiden: Brill, 1995.

———. "Prolegomenon to a Theory of Early Synagogue Development." In *Judaism in Late Antiquity*, edited by Alan J. Avery-Peck and Jacob Neusner, vol. 4, 121–54. Handbook of Oriental Studies: The Near and Middle East. Leiden: Brill, 2001.

Foerster, Gideon. "The Synagogues at Masada and Herodium." In *Ancient Synagogues Revealed*, edited by Lee I. Levine. Jerusalem: Israel Exploration Society, 1981.

Jastrow, Marcus. *A Dictionary of the Targumim, the Talmud Babli and Yerushalmi, and the Midrashic Literature*. New York: Judaica Press, 1996.

Josephus. *Jewish Antiquities*. Translated Ralph Marcus. Loeb Classical Library. Cambridge, MA: Harvard University Press, 1963.

———. *The Jewish War*. Translated by H. St. J. Thackeray. Loeb Classical Library. London: Heinemann, 1927–1928.

Levine, Lee I. *The Ancient Synagogue. The First Thousand Years*. New Haven: Yale University Press, 2000.

———. "The First-Century Synagogue: Critical Reassessments and Assessments of the Critical." In *Religion and Society in Roman Palestine: Old Questions, New Approaches*, edited by Douglas R. Edwards, 70–102. New York: Routledge, 2001.

Matassa, Lidia. "On the Identification of Pre-70 C.E. Synagogues in the Land of Israel." PhD diss., Trinity College Dublin, 2010.

Netzer, Ehud. *Greater Herodium*. Qedem: Monographs of the Institute of Archaeology. Jerusalem: Hebrew University, 1981.

———. "Herodium." *The New Encyclopedia of Archaeological Excavations in the Holy Land*. Vol. 2. Edited by Ephraim Stern. Jerusalem: Israel Exploration Society and Carta, 1993.

———. *The Architecture of Herod, the Great Builder*. Tübingen: Mohr/Siebeck, 2006.

Patrich, Joseph. "Corbo's Excavations at Herodium." *Israel Exploration Journal* 42 (1992) 241–45.

Spijkerman, Augusto. *Herodion III. Catologo delle Monete*. Pubblicazioni dello Studium Biblicum Franciscanum 20/3. Jerusalem: Franciscan Printing Press, 1972.

Testa, Emmanuele. *Herodion IV. I Graffiti e Gli Ostraka*. Pubblicazioni dello Studium Biblicum Franciscanum 20/4. Jerusalem: Franciscan Printing Press, 1972.

3

Gender and Syro-Palestinian Archaeology
A Post-Feminist Perspective

Cynthia Shafer-Elliott

INTRODUCTION

THERE ARE NUMEROUS ARCHAEOLOGICAL frameworks, or methodologies, to choose from when engaging in archaeological research. In fact, there seem to be new types developed fairly regularly, which, on the one hand can be seen as good thing, for one must always be stretching one's mind and the limits of archaeology; on the other hand, it can been seen as archaeological theory run amok, with new theories being introduced whenever an archaeologist so inclines. When engaging in archaeological research, it is easy for one to feel as though they must wade through the aisles of the archaeological methodology superstore and pick from the vast selection of approaches that best suits one's needs. The theories that line the fictitious superstore aisles, however, are often chosen as a result of familiarity and comfort with little critical evaluation.

One such method is gender archaeology, which has evolved within the last two to three decades from a backwater soapbox for feminists to a recognized discipline within the greater archaeology community. Many female, and some male, archaeologists have found a voice in gender archaeology while helping the forgotten women of the past be heard. Regardless of the good it has done, gender archaeology needs to be critically evaluated like any other archaeological theory. I am aware that the term "post-feminist" in my title brings with it some amount of uncertainty. It seems that there is no consensus as to what post-feminism is, let alone what it does. Some feminists see post-feminism as the announcement that feminism is no longer needed, that it has accomplished its goals, or is an out-right rejection of them. Others see it as encouraging feminists to get off their backside, get to it, and quit whining.[1] Still yet, others see the "post" in post-feminism as denoting time and order, not rejection. In fact, they see post-feminism as a pluralistic view that is concerned with disturbing universals, the same universals that are at the heart of post-modernism and encourages a certain viewpoint of multiple truths, roles, and realities. Therefore, post-feminism could be seen as in alignment to post-modernism; this is the definition of post-feminism used in this research.[2]

This definition does not indicate that this all-accepting embrace of post-feminism has made critical analysis passé. Indeed, while this definition of post-feminism, like post-modernism, is accepting of all interpretations, it also encourages the demystifying of past and modern constructions. So, if deconstruction (for lack of a better word) is encouraged, what is prohibiting us from demystifying some of the newer constructions that have emerged from post-modernism/post-feminism? Post-feminist approaches to archaeology call us, rather requires us, to examine the methods one chooses to use in research, even if the method is one that is generally supported by the post-feminist theory itself, such as gender. As an egalitarian and feminist, I find looking critically at gendered archaeology in general, and more specifically, at gendered Syro-Palestinian archaeology, as a bit disloyal. Nevertheless, as an archaeologist I must admit my concerns with gendered Syro-Palestinian archaeology when I ask of it some tough questions, and this paper is a direct result of such inquiry.

The purpose of this paper is to examine whether or not Syro-Palestinian archaeology can be engendered, even from a post-feminist perspective. I will begin by providing a brief description of what gender archaeology is, how one "does" gender archaeology, the pros and cons of such an approach, followed by my present conclusion, which, as anyone

---

1. Piepmeir, "Post Feminism vs. The Third Wave."
2. Perhaps a better description of my perspective could be defined as egalitarian.

who has truly been effected by post-feminism would say, I have the right to change (!).

GENDER ARCHAEOLOGY

What is Gender Archaeology?

Gender archaeology was birthed from the so-called "second-wave" feminist movement of the 1960's and the subsequent rise of feminist archaeology. Out of its basic themes there is only one proper practice or application of feminist archaeology to actual archaeological remains—that is the examination of gender in the archaeological record, which has thus become known as gender archaeology. Sarah Milledge Nelson defines gender archaeology as research that "considers people in the past, especially the relationships of women and men to the social, economic, political, and ideological structures of particular societies."[3] A common misconception is that, because of its genesis and connections to feminist archaeology, gender archaeology consists only of women archaeologists studying women, an issue Carol Meyers so clearly contests by stating that:

> Although the term gender is sometimes used, or suspected of being used, as a code word for women, gendered archaeology in fact informs the past lives of men as well as women. Because people rarely lived gender-segregated lives, learning about the one gender provides information about the other. Moreover, arguing for a gendered archaeology becomes, in a sense, an argument for an archaeology of people—an archaeology that can go beyond the artifacts and structures and seek to recover the texture of the lives of those who used them.[4]

One of the issues feminist/gender archaeology has, and is trying to rectify, is that archaeology and history in the past has been androcentric, or male-centered. Traditionally, histories were written by elite urban males for other elite urban males;[5] likewise, archaeological sites and their material culture were primarily excavated and interpreted by male archaeologists for other male archaeologists. While feminist archaeol-

---

3. Nelson, *Gender in Archaeology: Analyzing Power and Prestige*, 17.
4. Meyers, "Engendering Syro-Palestinian Archaeology," 185.
5. Meyers, *Discovering Eve*, 11–13.

ogy and, consequently, gender archaeology may have begun as a means of reclaiming the forgotten women of the past, it has evolved to include the forgotten men and children of the past as well. Indeed, if elite urban males wrote most of history, it must be recognized that their version of history not only excludes women but also excludes the non-elite and/or rural men of those same societies. The same observation can be applied to archaeology; if most of archaeology was androcentric in its approach and practice and was concerned with the big, monumental sites and artifacts, it can be assumed that those whose lives and material culture did not fall into those categories were largely ignored. Hence, gendered archaeology is seen by some as an important methodology to employ regardless of the agenda or focus of the excavation because it is concerned with the men, women, and children of all societies in time and space.

How Is Gendered Archaeology Implemented?

An important aspect in the implementation of gender archaeology is the differentiation between the terms sex and gender. "Sex" refers to the biological differences between males and females, while "gender" refers to the socially constructed roles of males and females in particular societies or groups; sex is physical while gender is taught. Sarah Milledge Nelson writes that, "Certain roles, activities, or behaviors are assigned to particular people grouped together as a gender. Thus gender is related to sex, but is not the same thing."[6] Gender archaeology focuses on taught gender roles that may or may not be related to the biological aspect of sex, which can vary between cultures, and change through time.

Archaeology in general, and Syro-Palestinian archaeology in particular, has historically focused on the macro, or the big, monumental people, places, things, and events that hardly reflect the every day life of ancient Israelites or Judahites. Instead, a focus on the micro, or the small, traditionally considered insignificant people, places, things, and events should be employed if the every day life of both average and elite men, women and children are to be found.[7] Gender archaeology is the study of the socially constructed roles, activities, or behaviors of ancient men and women, both common and elite. The inclusion of gender studies helps to clarify the relationship between the material remains and activity areas

---

6. Nelson, *Gender in Archaeology*, 15.
7. Meyers, "Engendering Syro-Palestinian Archaeology," 187.

with the actual activities, those who participated in those activities, and the behaviors behind those activities.

Strategies for implementing gender archaeology mirror feminist archaeology while adding new ingredients to the cupboard. First is the critique of androcentrism, which is the awareness of and exposing the historically male-biased interpretation of gender.

Second is ethnographic and ethnoarchaeological observation. Ethnography is the "study of contemporary cultures through direct observation," while ethnoarchaeology is the observation of contemporary cultures in order to understand "the behaviors and relationships that underlie the production and use of the material culture."[8]

Iconography is the visual representation, in various modes of media (such as figurines, frescos, and mosaics), of men, women, and children and the activities in which they engaged.

Pertinent texts can provide an abundance of information on gender, gender relationships, and gender activities that members of a society engaged or were idealized as being engaged.

Gender related factors could be gleaned from burials and human remains in numerous ways including the employment of DNA and bone analysis to human remains to determine sex differentials in workload, physical risk, disease, nutrition, reproductive patterns, childhood stress, trauma, and mortality.[9]

Spatial arrangements and households are given special attention because it is recognized that the majority of daily activities occurred within the dwelling unit, or household. The spatial analysis of the dwelling and the material culture found within or around the dwelling provides a stage for the routine of daily activities and performances that could lead to an awareness of the practices of gendered lives.[10] In spite of this being a strategy for implementing gender archaeology, the focus on the household and its spatial arrangements has become a separate framework of analysis called household archaeology.[11]

The analysis of artifacts is considered essential to the study of gender in archaeology because material culture is seen as "intimately

---

8. Ibid.
9. Nelson, *Gender in Archaeology*, 59.
10. Sørensen, "Gender, Things, and Material Culture," 121.
11. Hardin, "Understanding Domestic Space."

involved in the construction of meaning."[12] A gender-sensitive approach leads to the assumption of the activities behind the artifacts and consequently the people who participated in those activities. Gender attribution, or the linking of artifacts with gender, is the primary mode of combining the physical material culture with gender. By assuming the activity associated with artifact, gender is attributed to the activity and thus the people who engaged in that activity.[13] This is a problematic assumption, as we will see.

PROS AND CONS OF GENDER ARCHAEOLOGY

The benefits of engendering Syro-Palestinian archaeology have been alluded to earlier, but require further mention here in order to balance the arguments of doubt. There are two main reasons why gender archaeology is seen as a productive member of the archaeology community: one, it is interdisciplinary in nature; and two, it promotes the study of daily life.

A post-feminist approach to archaeology recognizes that archaeology is a conglomerate field—a discipline that is made up of different fields or parts that are grouped together to form a whole but remain distinct entities. In other words, archaeology is intricately connected to numerous disciplines such as linguistics, science, and history, used in tandem to study the past. Interdisciplinary approaches allow for interpretations that are more varied and new and different perspectives that may not have been found otherwise. Discourse between various disciplines, such as gender and archaeology, could enhance our understanding of the past.

Secondly, gender archaeology focuses more on the daily life of ancient societies. As was mentioned earlier, historically, Syro-Palestinian archaeologists have focused on stratigraphic concerns and the macro, or the monumental places, structures, and material culture, such as temples, palaces, and fortifications. Carol Myers writes that, "Monumental architecture produced by male-dominated public elites (monarchies, priesthoods and the military) has traditionally been more attractive to archaeologists—and their supporters—than have been the less opulent

---

12. Sørensen, "Gender, Things, and Material Culture," 105.

13. Ibid., 113. Milledge Nelson provides this list of strategies for implementing gender archaeology in *Gender in Archaeology*, 56–62.

or visually striking remnants of daily lives of the peasant populations of Near Eastern antiquity."[14]

Some Syro-Palestinian archaeologists, and those who fund them, are attracted to *Eretz Israel* and its connection with the Bible, which is perfectly acceptable until it begins to dominate the focus and course of the excavation. With the Bible in one hand and a trowel in the other, some have directed their excavations to link sites and their material culture with the people and events in the biblical text. Problems with this approach are two-fold. First, the Bible and trowel approach does not allow archaeology to perform as its own discipline nor does it allow the material culture to speak, per se, for itself. Secondly, the Bible and trowel approach only allows for one perspective, that of the elite urban males who wrote and redacted the biblical text, thus ignoring the majority of the ancient Israelite and Judahite men and women whose very lives the archaeologist is excavating.

Arguments for engendering Syro-Palestinian archaeology are strong and noble in their intentions. However, we must recognize the faults of such an effort as well as its strengths. The primary fault of gender archaeology is also one of its strengths: its interdisciplinary nature. It is this very nature that unbalances the engendered approach by being overly dependent upon other disciplines. If gender is defined as socially constructed roles of males and females in particular societies or groups, then this description begets the question: Do social constructs, like gender, leave a physical presence behind? Although gender archaeology claims to be dependent upon material culture, the obvious must be stated—material culture itself is not gendered. Pots, weaving loom weights, architecture, weapons, etc.: gender is associated with these and other artifacts, but they themselves are not gendered. The only categories of material culture that could possibly be classified as gendered is that of iconography or burial remains due to the fact that both are physical remains that could reflect sex and gender; the latter should be narrowed to actual skeletal remains, not necessarily the artifacts buried with the dead since "burials reflect gender ideologies, which may or may not coincide with actual practice . . ."[15] Unfortunately, both icons (in their various forms) and skeletal remains are a rare occurrence in Iron Age Syro-Palestinian archaeology.

---

14. Meyers, "Engendering Syro-Palestinian Archaeology," 186.
15. Brumfiel, "Methods in Feminist and Gender Archaeology," 39.

Consequently, gender-sensitive archaeologists must turn to other forms of evidence, like the attribution of gender in artifacts.

Unlike iconography and skeletal remains, the attribution of gender is not based solely on the object, but on what is "behind" the object. The assumption of gendered activities is risky because the activity behind the artifact is not gendered either; rather, it is the social value behind the activity, which is behind the artifact, that is gendered. In other words, the concept of gender attribution claims that if the socially constructed meaning of gender is behind the activity, both the activity and the artifact are gendered.

In order to find the social value behind the activity, archaeologists are dependent upon analogies—an assertion that Carol Meyers readily admits: "Although the persons are no longer visible and the material culture itself is not gendered, usually the activities are gendered . . . through a series of analytical steps involving ethnographic, iconographic and ethnohistorical data, gender can be attributed to those activities."[16]

In order to implement gender archaeology, it must be recognized that it is a methodology that leans heavily on other disciplines, such as ethnography, ethnoarchaeology, and ethnohistory. These analogies can be extremely helpful when attempting to clarify say, the use of an artifact, but to depend upon them as the foundation for an archaeological argument, even a gender-sensitive one, is questionable at best. Furthermore, there are other concerns regarding the use of these analogous tools, which Sarah Milledge Nelson describes as the "awareness of the effects of colonialism, of the bias of the ethnographer, of environmental change . . . [and] we must avoid assuming that the past of recent cultures are relics of a stagnant or pristine past."[17] These are legitimate concerns that must be accounted for when utilizing these analogies in any study; but to establish the foundation of an archaeological argument almost solely on analogies is being disingenuous, regardless how noble the quest.

While sensitivity to gender is helpful in focusing on the micro dimension, or daily life, it must be kept in mind that gender cannot be directly observed through material remains. Archaeologies are first and foremost based on physical remains and must be accountable to interpretations based on those physical remains.

---

16. Meyers, "Engendering Syro-Palestinian Archaeology," 186; italics mine.
17. Nelson, *Gender in Archeology*, 56.

CONCLUSION

The degree of doubt in our ability to engender Syro-Palestinian archaeology is troubling; however, there is hope at the end of the proverbial tunnel. As a means of enhancing its reliability, gender archaeology should promote a greater dependency on the actual physical remains and less on analogies. Utilizing iconography and scientific inquiry of skeletal remains (when available) as a more physical representation of gender and gendered activities would be a step in this direction.

Iconography, or representational art, can provide a glimpse into the appearance, the daily activities, and the negotiation of gender that took place within a given society. However, there are some issues that need to be kept in mind when analyzing representational art: occasionally, the figures represented do not display any anatomical features or dress that would indicate differences in sex or gender; this could cause confusion when attempting to clarify the gender roles of a particular society. Furthermore, if the representation is found within a public setting, the possibility must be recognized that perhaps it was used by societal authorities to enforce gender norms, or as an artistic expression of ideology. Thirdly, iconographic remains need to be contemporaneous and from the same culture. Regardless of these questions, representational art provides the archaeologist with the opportunity to investigate "the negotiation of gender" even within different societal contexts, such as public, state-sponsored art or private, domestic art.[18]

Bioarchaeology, or the study of human skeletal material remains from archaeological contexts, provides reliable methods for determining the sex, and possibly gendered roles, of skeletal remains based on their measurements.[19] Brumfiel writes, "many types of behavior leave their marks on human bone. Since gender is socially constructed, it must be created and maintained through engendering performances, and these habitual performance result in skeletal alterations ... Human bone is the closest thing that archaeologists have to the direct observation of gendered behavior in the [prehistoric] past.[20]

Once the sexing of the remains has been accomplished, evidence for differential gender-related factors can be examined from the remains,

---

18. Brumfiel, "Methods in Feminist and Gender Archaeology," 40–41.
19. Ibid., 37.
20. Ibid.

including: "pathologies, repetitive stress markers with respect to type and degree of bone deformation, nutritional stress, demographic representation in the burial record, differential care, osteological markers related to fertility, the movement of people, and dietary isotope analysis."[21] If the preservation of the skeletal remains is sufficient then a great deal of information regarding gender roles of a particular society can be revealed without being completely dependent upon ethnographic analogy. For example, repetitive stress markers on female skeletons found in the Near East demonstrate characteristic deformation of knees and shoulders due to hours spent grinding on stone mortars.[22]

Unfortunately, burial remains are hard to find, especially in ancient Israel and Judah. But all is not lost; gender archaeology can still be implemented by applying some basic principles: several strands of data must point in the same direction; coupling any physical remains that are actual enactments of gender (such as skeletal remains and iconography) with the representations of gender (such as gender attribution of artifacts and ethnographic analogies) that indicate a consistent view of gendered activities and behaviors could be effective. Third, a case must be made for employing gender attribution to artifacts for each historical task, as well as using artifacts found in use contexts as opposed to artifacts found in rubbish piles or storage.[23]

In the end, I must conclude that together, these various strands of evidence have the potential to provide valuable information on the gender-specific activities and behaviors of ancient societies. However, a gender-sensitive approach to archaeology should be cautiously implemented with an awareness that the inferring of gender-related activities and behaviors based on physical remains alone is on somewhat shaky ground. This proves to be even more difficult when attempting to apply material remains based on gender archaeology to Iron II Judah, which has little iconography and skeletal remains. It would be more prudent to employ an archaeological methodology that is founded on actual physical remains and utilize a gender-sensitive approach as a secondary framework.

---

21. Arnold, "Gender and Archaeological Mortuary Analysis," 147–49.
22. Ibid., 147.
23. Brumfiel, "Methods in Feminist and Gender Archaeology," 43.

BIBLIOGRAPHY

Arnold, Bettina. "Gender and Archaeological Mortuary Analysis." In *Handbook of Gender in Archaeology*, edited by Sarah Milledge Nelson, 137–70. Gender and Archaeology Series. New York: Alta Mira, 2006.

Brumfiel, Elizabeth M. "Methods in Feminist and Gender Archaeology: A Feeling for Difference—and Likeness." In *Handbook of Gender in Archaeology*, edited by Sarah Milledge Nelson, 31–58. Gender and Archaeology Series. New York: Alta Mira Press, 2006.

Conkey, Margaret W., and Joan M. Gero. "Tensions, Pluralities, and Engendering Archaeology: An Introduction to Women and Prehistory." In *Engendering Archaeology: Women and Prehistory*, edited by Joan M. Gero and Margaret W. Conkey, 3–30. Social Archaeology Series. Oxford: Blackwell, 1991.

Hardin, James W. "Understanding Domestic Space: An Example from Iron Age Tel Halif." *Near Eastern Archaeology* 67 (2004) 71–83.

Hodder, Ian. *Reading the Past: Current Approaches to Interpretation in Archaeology*. Cambridge: Cambridge University Press, 1986.

———. *Theory and Practice in Archaeology*. Material Cultures Series. London: Routledge, 1992.

Johnson, Matthew. *Archaeological Theory: An Introduction*. Oxford: Blackwell, 1999.

Meyers, Carol. *Discovering Eve: Ancient Israelite Women in Context*. Oxford: Oxford University Press, 1988.

Meyers, Carol. "Engendering Syro-Palestinian Archaeology: Reasons and Resources." *Near Eastern Archaeology* 66 (2003) 185–197.

Nelson, Sarah Milledge. *Gender in Archaeology: Analyzing Power and Prestige*. Walnut Creek, CA: Alta Mira, 1997.

Piepmeir, Alison. "Post Feminism vs. The Third Wave." No pages. Online: http:// www.electronicbookreview.com/thread/writingpostfeminism/reconfiguredrip2

Schiffer, Michael Brian. *Behavioral Archaeology*. Foundations of Archaeological Inquiry Series. Salt Lake City: University of Utah Press, 1995.

Sørensen, Marie Louise. *Gender Archaeology*. Cambridge: Polity Press, 2000.

———. "Gender, Things, and Material Culture." In *Handbook of Gender in Archaeology*, edited by Sarah Milledge Nelson, 105–35. Gender and Archaeology Series. New York: Alta Mira, 2006.

Spector, Janet D., and Margaret W. Conkey. "Archaeology and the Study of Gender." In *Advances in Archaeological Method and Theory*, edited by Michael B. Schiffer, 1–38. New York: Academic Press, 1984.

Wylie, Alison. "Gender Theory and the Archaeological Record: Why is There No Archaeology of Gender?" In *Engendering Archaeology: Women and Prehistory*, edited by Joan M. Gero and Margaret W. Conkey, 31–54. Social Archaeology Series. Oxford: Blackwell, 1991.

4

Reconsidering Jacob

A Gendered Approach to Genesis 25:19–34

Trisha Tschopp

INTRODUCTION

Feminist approaches to the Hebrew Bible have generally concentrated on reconstructing life within a patriarchal system by analyzing and elucidating the role of women within its context. Interest in women's roles in Biblical Studies has generated valuable research and discussion within the past thirty years, undoubtedly owing its impetus to second-wave feminism of the 1960s and 1970s. In regards to methodology, Esther Fuchs has noted three major trajectories of contemporary feminist study of the Hebrew Bible:

- attempting to recover women's "authentic cultures and voices" through historical and literary perspectives, focusing on how "women have changed history, created their own rituals and practices, and followed their goddesses whether as marginal practices or in the dead center of male monotheism."

- acknowledging that the Bible was "composed by and about men," yet arguing its multivalent, multifaceted representations of women's lives, due to women found in both the influential and submissive spheres. "Women's roles transcend simple stereotypes, offering a diversity of images and a variety of authentic voices."

- arguing that the Bible is "a patriarchal compilation, giving voice to patriarchal institutional practices and endorsing the social and symbolic supremacy of men"; creating "the sexual categories and hierarchies that its many readers take for granted"; and "endorsing desirable forms of behavior and that is has contributed to the way contemporary womanhood is defined in both religious and secular contexts."[1]

Although these perspectives vary, they share what Phyllis Trible recognizes as a "hermeneutical challenge . . . to translate biblical faith without sexism," and coincidentally, without eisegesis.[2] Like other interdisciplinary studies, instead of relying on a binary, "either/or" interpretation of biblical material, research within feminist Biblical Studies adopts a "yes/and" interpretation, recognizing that there may be more than one way of viewing a text. It is within this framework (and subsequently aligning myself with Fuch's middle-ground, second approach to feminist biblical scholarship) that I would like to suggest an alternative way of viewing Gen 25:19–34. Although traditionally viewed as an eponymous narrative representing the complicated relationship and rivalry between Jacob (Israel) and Esau (Edom/Rome), I believe it also functions as "de-patriarchalizing" Jacob who acts as the primary female figure within this particular passage. In other words, the part that Jacob plays during this short narrative blurs traditionally assigned gender roles by allowing Jacob to remain biologically male while he seems to fulfill a traditional "female" social role in early Israel. Coincidentally, it is not until after his birthright is secured (in Genesis 27) that we see Jacob emerge as a typical "male" social figure. This is seen especially in comparison with his/her counterpart, Esau, where precisely the female social role justifies trickery and an exploitation of weakness as an acceptable method of gaining power or position.

CONSTRUCTING GENDER IN THE ANCIENT NEAR EAST

Gender roles are not biologically determined, but rather a product of particular personal experience(s). It is true that there are "individual psychological processes in addition to, and in a different register from, culture, language, and power relations that construct gender for the individual.

---

1. Fuchs, "Feminist Approaches to the Hebrew Bible," 77–79.
2. Trible, "Depatriarchalizing in Biblical Interpretation," 31.

Meaning—at least about any linguistic or cultural categories that matter to us—is always psychologically particular to the individual."[3] This idea of gender as a cultural, social, and personal construct—not a stereotype—chips away at the perception that there is a clear bifurcation of characteristics belonging to either the masculine or the feminine realm. The interplay between these relative elements in producing new, meaningful readings of a work bolster support for the reader-response theory within literary criticism, and similar methods of textual study. However, almost paradoxically, definitive and universal themes need to be acknowledged before engaging in a serious dialogue about gender, culture, and social issues. In addition, problems arise when considering that the stages of examining and researching gender roles for ancient Israel are in its infancy, and as David Clines writes in his study on David and the construction of masculinity in ancient Israel that, "none of the Bible dictionaries, for example, broaches this fundamental cultural subject, though they are packed with trivia about the material culture of the world of the Bible. We have to start more or less from scratch."[4]

REBEKAH AND THE 'BIRTH OF A HERO PARADIGM'

Regarding attempts to reconstruct the mores of the ancient Near Eastern world, and even extending to contemporary psychoanalytic feminist critique, scholars have traditionally focused on two specific aspects to define the role of women: heterosexuality through a relationship with their husband, and a concern for childbearing and motherhood.[5] Indeed, we see Rebekah satisfying both requirements in Gen 25:19–26. In these short verses, Rebekah is identified both as Isaac's "wife" (Gen 25:21) and as a mother when she fulfills her ascribed "womanly duties"—conceiving, giving birth, and producing two sons (25:21b–24). As a barren woman divinely transformed to give birth to the future patriarchal leader Jacob, Rebekah prominently plays a role in initiating a familiar literary motif and what Robert Alter refers to as a "type-scene . . . [occurring] not in the rituals of daily existence but at the crucial junctures in the lives of the

---

3. Chodorow, "Gender as a Personal and Cultural Construction," 517.

4. Clines, *Interested Parties*, 13–14.

5. For an interesting discussion of determining the social identity from the 1900s to the present, see Breyfogle, "The Social Status of Woman in the Old Testament." Contrasted with a more modern look at the flexibility of gender constructs, see Chodorow, "Gender as a Personal and Cultural Construction."

heroes, from conception and birth to betrothal to death bed."[6] Athalya Brenner expands on this particular type-scene, as she specifically outlines the "Birth of a Hero" paradigm, though it must be noted that this paradigm is not in itself a "unique pattern exclusive to biblical literature."[7] The model is outlined as such (and annotated with verses germane to this model):

1. A woman, preferably of noble origin (Gen 25:20–21a)
2. is barren (until quite an advanced age) / variations on this theme are possible, as long as they deal with pre-conception difficulties (Gen 25:21–22)
3. The woman has a divine revelation in which the future birth is announced (Gen 25:23)
4. Sometimes the son's fate in early or later years is alluded to (Gen 25:23; 26)

Using Brenner's model, Rebekah falls into the category of a single mother possessing two sons or more, and functions: "not to emphasize her own social status against other women, encouraging a competitive atmosphere in a race to produce biologically male-heirs (as seen later in Genesis ch. 30 with Rachel and Leah). Rather, [participates in] a monogamous (contrasted with polygamous) relationship, that produces children from a barren state, anticipate the births as rivals, for a number of features point to their being a contrasted pair."[8]

Brenner typically considers women within this category to possess strong, distinct personalities (such as Naomi, Ruth, Elizabeth, or Mary); however, I believe that Rebekah remains rather one-dimensional within this particular narrative.[9] Her identity hinges on Bethuel and Laban (v. 20), Isaac (v. 20–21), or her male children (v. 24). Instead of her initiating contact with the Divine, Isaac pleads on her behalf (v. 21). Similarly, in her only independent action of inquiry to the Deity, the place remains unnamed, and her voice remains etymologically muffled. Gerhard von Rad

---

6. Alter, *Art of Biblical Narrative*, 51.
7. Brenner, "Female Social Behaviour," 258–59.
8. Ibid., 269–70.
9. Surely, it can be argued that her "strong, distinct personality" emerges in Genesis 27, as she guides Jacob through obtaining the birthright; however, I am more concerned with examining her function within this short narrative.

notes: "Judged as a narrative, however, this report is remarkably without vividness. The prayers to Yahweh (in vv. 21 and 22b) are simply asserted, but not related. The place is not named (there must have been a cultic center to which Rebekah 'went'), nor are any details of this event described more closely. Only God's saying is given verbatim."[10]

Although Rebekah's phrase is recorded, it remains enigmatic. E. A. Speiser writes that most translators lean towards a phrasing like "why do I live?" following the Syriac, with an eye toward Gen 27:46. But, a closer parallel is found in v. 32, as "what good is . . . " and Rebekah proceeds to consult Yahweh through an oracle ". . . which shows that, though desperate, she was not as yet resigned to her fate."[11] Thus, despite Rebekah fulfilling her biological duties as a female character, her social position is secondary (or non-existent) to the principal goal of bringing about children, and as soon as this requirement is met, she drops out of focus.[12] Indeed, this emphasis on motherhood is not necessarily advocating an elevated place in Israelite society for altruistic measure. Fuchs notes that, "valuing mothers is not in and of itself a symptom of approval or a trace of ancient feminism. Motherhood insures the viability of patrilineal genealogy in a precarious world. It is, therefore, vital to the functioning biblical patriarchy, which promotes women to the extent that they contribute to or promote its success."[13]

Rebekah conforms to the two quantifiable characteristics attributed by scholars determining gender; however, there must be more (yet tacit) characteristics that denote female social roles within ancient Israel—if anything else, to avoid paradigms becoming stereotypes. Carol Meyers adds that, "except for the biologically determined roles of childbearing and suckling, there is virtually no universal assignation of any specific societal role to one particular sex. This striking plasticity of gender behavior has, in fact, been the basis of arguments for non-biological determination of sex-role behaviors."[14]

---

10. Von Rad, *Genesis*, 259–60.

11. Speiser, *Genesis*, 194.

12. That is, until the evanescent mention that "Rebekah loved Jacob" in v. 28; of course, the narrator chooses to reintroduce her in Genesis 27.

13. Fuchs, "Feminist Approaches to the Hebrew Bible," 82.

14. Meyers, "Procreation, Production, and Protection," 572.

SETTING THE SCENE: DWELLING IN TENTS

Discussing biblical narrative seems to require an eye for detail, and requires actively seeking to observe details hidden within the terse style. In comparing the narrative styles of Homeric Epic and the Sacrifice of Isaac (or *Akedah*) in Genesis 22, Erich Auerbach writes regarding biblical stories that:

> they are fraught with "background" and mysterious, containing a second, concealed meaning ... the tendency to a smoothing down and harmonizing events to a simplification of motives, to a static definition of characters which avoids conflict, vacillation, and development, such as are natural to the legendary structure, does not predominate in the Old Testament world of legend. Abraham, Jacob, or even Moses produces a more concrete, direct, and historical impression than the figures of the Homeric world—not because they are better described in terms of sense (the contrary is the case) but because the confused, contradictory multiplicity of events; the psychological and factual cross-purposes, which true history reveals, have not disappeared in the representation but still remain clearly perceptible.[15]

Noting the multilayered, complex narrative that is "fraught with background," it may seem trite to state that what the audience perceives of Jacob and Esau is only what the omniscient narrator tells the audience.[16] As mentioned previously, the verses featuring the "Birth of a Hero" paradigm (Gen 25:21–26) are seemingly suspended out of a locale—without references to cultic temples or domestic spheres.[17] The emphasis is not necessarily where the event of the births took place—simply that there are contrasting differences between the children.[18] Beginning in Gen 25:27, the narrator establishes the setting by referring to the contrasting ele-

---

15. Auerbach, *Mimesis*, 16–20.

16. Historical-critical approaches may chide me as viewing this section as a closed, literary unit, seeing as it is an amalgam of the Priestly source (typically viewed as vv. 19–20, and v. 26b) and the Yahwistic source (21–26a; 27–34); however, my analysis involves viewing the text as a final product, assuming the texts were joined together for a purpose (be it theological or aesthetic).

17. For a more comprehensive discussion of this, please see Hendel, *Epic of the Patriarch*, 38–40.

18. Alter, *Genesis*, 126.

ments of each character utilizing parallelism, the technique used mostly in biblical poetry, thereby setting up a linguistic contrast.[19]

Verse 27a and b mirror each other in regards to its syntax, and provide a point of reference when Esau "comes in from the field" (v. 29) to meet Jacob, the tent-dweller. Primarily, the domain of a woman's activities was the household, where she exercised authority in her role,[20] and it is no doubt surprising that Jacob is listed within its realm. Typically, it is women who are generally depicted as tent-dwellers. With regards to the Patriarchs seen before Jacob within Genesis, Abraham is depicted as outside the tent opening when he receives three visitors, as compared to Sarah as inside (Gen 17:21–22); Isaac is depicted as "in the field" (similar to Esau) when Rebekah notices him, and he brings her "into the tent of Sarah" where she is initiated into the Matriarchy (Gen 24:66). The phrasing for Jacob as a "dweller of tents" (ישב אהלים) is only otherwise found in another Yahwistic piece in Gen 4:20, referring to Jabal as the ancestor of "those who dwell in tents and amidst herds." Tracing this back to Jabal and the Yahwistic reference to Israel's pastoral-nomadic etiology seems to be the motive behind viewing Jacob as a pastoral figure contrasted by Esau's savagery. However, placing the narrative within a tent(s) seems to contain embedded feminine qualities. Don Seeman argues that "The interiority of biblical women does not necessarily describe ancient social reality. Rather, it indicates a concern with certain qualities—fecundity, vulnerability, and intimacy, among others—that are indexed by the use of interior metaphors. The depiction of men as they enter women's tents, therefore, indicates a larger narrative preoccupation with these qualities, which are central to biblical representations of gender and nationhood."[21]

Regardless, if this is supposed to signify a cultural reality or an allusion to fertility and vulnerability, the result is the same—there is a blurring of gender boundaries regarding what belongs in the "female" domain by referring to Jacob as a "tent-dweller" in Gen 25:27. Strikingly, however, Jacob is not always referred to as a "dweller in tents"; in Gen 30:16, Jacob (like Esau in Gen 25:19) came in "from the field" (and Leah, in attempting to control the situation goes "out" of the tent to meet him). Thus, it is only after in Genesis 30 (after he secures the birthright, and wrestling with

---

19. Collins, *Short Introduction to the Hebrew Bible*, 239–40.
20. King and Stager, *Life in Biblical Israel*, 49.
21. Seeman, "'Where Is Sarah Your Wife?'" 106.

a divinity-type at Beth-el), when he emerges from the tent and into the field—initiating a change in the power dynamic.

ESAU AS THE "WILD MAN"

To understand the interplay of social gender roles, the character of Esau must be examined. The construction of Esau is rooted in biblical and ancient Near Eastern allusion, as his description seems to bolster support for associating him with the "wild man" character—"a stock character of international folklore tradition."[22] Gregory Mobley notes that "the most distinctive physical characteristic of the medieval wild man is hairiness."[23] Thus, it seems since birth Esau is destined to fulfill this role, as even the folk etymology of his name denotes his "hairy reputation" by playing on the Hebrew word שער ("hairy") as a tenuous connection to שעיר, a synonym of Edom.[24] The depiction of Esau is comparable to that of Enkidu (another "wild man" figure), as the child emerges with "a hairy mantle all over," which is almost the same as the phrase "shaggy with hair was his whole body," applied to Enkidu in Gilgamesh Tablet I, column ii, line 36 (where the phrase šu'ur šarta is cognate with Hebrew שער).[25] As James Kugel notes, "The narrative mentions Esau's 'furriness' in order to prepare us for a later detail in the story: Esau's hairy arms will ultimately help Jacob deceive his blind father . . . Esau's hairiness becomes symbolic of his animal nature; he is little better than a beast of prey himself."[26]

Similarly, the word used to describe Esau as "red" (אדמוני) is otherwise only attributed to David before he is anointed King in the midst of his brothers (1 Sam 16:12) or when he is battling Goliath (1 Sam 17:42). Typically, this is translated as "red" or "ruddy"[27] and is generally thought to refer to the color of the skin, but it may be the color of the hair.[28] Similarly, Susan Niditch elaborates on the theme of hair denoting masculinity in her treatment of Samson, saying that "Freudian treatments of hair symbolism points to the universal association between hair and sexuality; the

---

22. Mobley, "Wild Man."
23. Ibid., 218.
24. Speiser, *Genesis*, 193.
25. Ibid., 196.
26. Kugel, *How to Read the Bible*, 137.
27. BDB, 10.
28. Clines, *Interested Parties*, 11.

hair is often a symbolic substitute for the genitals or for sexual potency, or a manifestation of sexuality ... the cutting of Samson's hair, ironically accomplished by a woman's treachery, makes him into a woman, the subdued one, the defeated warrior."[29]

In linking this particular adjective with the future king of Israel, it also contributes to the literary technique of suspense by setting up the anticipation of Esau's dominance through his "masculinity," only to be foiled by the socially inferior Jacob by securing the birthright (vv. 31–34). Similarly, other traits shared by Esau and the Wild Man tradition are obvious. For example, a distinction of the Wild Man is "his kinship with nature, [knowing] about things that are unknown in human society."[30] It is clear that Esau is a "man of the field," who possessed intimate knowledge of the behavior of animals (v. 27). This knowledge, Mobley notes, is attractive to societies "who seek to capture wild men and somehow force them to divulge secrets."[31] The denotation of being a "man of the field" is the semantic equivalent of Akkadian *laḫmu*—the name of a particular figure in Mesopotamian art that represents the iconographic expression of the Wild Man.[32] In addition, the stereotypical Wild Man cannot talk coherently, and is literally, "a babbler."[33] Esau's direct speech to Jacob is crude and impatient, and "The famished brother cannot even come up with the ordinary Hebrew word for "stew" (נזיד) and instead points to the bubbling pot impatiently as (literally) "this red red." The verb he uses for gulping down occurs nowhere else in the Bible, but in Rabbinic Hebrew it is reserved for the feeding of animals ..."[34]

TRANSGRESSING GENDER BOUNDARIES: RECONSIDERING JACOB

Similar to the function of the "Birth of the Hero" paradigm that Rebekah exemplifies, or the "Wild Man Tradition" illustrated by Esau, I propose that the narrator intends for the audience to view Jacob as fulfilling the role of the "trickster" accented by fulfilling a female social role. The trickster

29. Niditch, "Samson as a Culture Hero, Trickster, and Bandit," 616–17.
30. Mobley, "Wild Man," 218.
31. Ibid.
32. Ibid., 223.
33. Ibid., 218.
34. Alter, *Genesis*, 129.

is also not unique to biblical literature, although many female characters within biblical literature are classified as tricksters (or temptresses), such as Tamar, Jael, and Rahab. The woman in ancient Israelite literature who would succeed almost must be a trickster: "[They] must follow the path typical of the marginalized . . . she seems to be the creation of a woman storyteller, one who is part of a male-centered world and is not in open rebellion against it, but who nevertheless subverts its rules . . . for this is also a woman's power in a man's world, a power of mockery, humor, and deception."[35]

In addition, the trickster need not be female, though "[a trickster] when a human being, he never ranks high, and his power lies in his witty brain or in some strange gift of nature."[36] In attempting to analyze the paradigm of the trickster, Niditch outlines a five-step trickster morphology:

1. problem: the hero has low status;
2. plan: a deception is schemed to improve status/condition;
3. execution: the plan is executed and results in an improved status/condition;
4. complication: the deception is uncovered; and
5. outcome: the hero subsequently experiences a reduction of status, but does survive.[37]

Niditch writes: "The raise in status for the heroes is followed by an unmasking of the plot, the deception, that helped them to achieve initial success. The plot revealed, the heroes' status is again reduced. The jig is up, but the protagonists survive to be involved in another plot, in the sense of both narrative and deception."[38]

By setting the scene in the woman's domain of the tent while tending to domestic duties, Jacob's perceived femininity contributes to Jacob's status as an "underdog" which excuses manipulating the situation to his/her advantage. Thus, although gender roles are a personal construct and

---

35. Newsom and Ringe, *Women's Bible Commentary*, 23.

36. Grottanelli, "Tricksters, Scape-Goats, Champions, Saviors," 120.

37. Summarized in Jackson, "Lot's Daughters and Tamar as Tricksters and the Patriarchal Narratives as Feminist Theology," 32. Originally from Niditch, *Underdogs and Tricksters*, especially 42–43.

38. Niditch, *Underdogs and Tricksters*, 44–45; also cited by Jackson, "Lot's Daughters," 32.

seemingly resist static definition, the politics of gender are "inevitably wrapped up with the ethos and aesthetics of power relations in general ... trickery can be categorized as a weapon of the weak, and thus quintessentially of women."[39]

Some may focus on Jacob's determination to secure the birthright as simply a quest to gain a double-portion inheritance, based primarily in a desire for increased property;[40] however, the primary purpose of the birthright denotes a change in social status within society, concomitantly inheriting authority. The laws of primogeniture "determines one's rank and status in kin-based society and in right of succession, whether as property owner, [or] as the head of the household (paterfamilias) ..."[41] In addition, S. H. Smith argues: "If Jacob is to usurp Esau's right to the Abrahamic promise, he must appropriate his procreative power. His quest to do this begins at the moment of birth when, symbolically, he seizes his brother by the genitals, the seat of procreation. From then on, Jacob, prompted by his mother, spares no effort to secure succession ..."[42]

Smith analyzes the etymological function of the Hebrew root ירך, and it is interesting to note that the references to Jacob's offspring is listed as springing from his loins or thighs (Gen 46:26; Exod 1:5) and subsequently is "intimately connected with the concept of procreation."[43] Jacob seems to actively pursue a social role that will elevate his role within society for the purpose of producing heirs/children, which as previously mentioned, is indicative of what modern scholars assign to the women's social/biological duty.

Oddly enough, it is the female social role that allows him to perform the "trick" to obtain the birthright; subtly, it is his biological function as a male that allows for him to maintain its possession. Tricksters are "notorious border crossers, [who] tend to elicit interpretive presumption and the possibility for misunderstanding."[44] It is not surprising then, that a biologically male character would be associated with female gender roles, complicating the "interpretive presumption" for the audience. As the plot

39. Mills, "Gender of the Trick," 240.
40. Kugel, *How to Read the Bible*, 140.
41. King and Stager, *Life in Biblical Israel*, 47–48.
42. Smith, "'Heel' and 'Thigh,'" 472.
43. Ibid., 469.
44. Monsma, "Active Readers ... Obverse Tricksters," 84.

thickens with Jacob cooking a stew, he is increasingly connected with the feminine realm. Life in biblical Israel generally required women to be responsible for providing food,[45] and it is precisely this cultivation of the woman's craft which seduces Esau to come in from the field, "famished" (v. 29). Esau, the "Wild Man" allows himself to be vulnerable by passing through the comfortable rustic setting, and subjects himself to a world unknown, and a world in which he does not hold authority. In verse 30, he entreats Jacob to give him the food that lured him in, using the Hebrew particle, נא,[46] which denotes the plea and significantly adds to the shift of power between Jacob and Esau. It should also be noted that it is typically women that play the primary agent in transforming the "Wild Man" archetype into a man of culture.[47] Jacob's tactics thus far bring Esau into a more urbane environment than that of the "openness," and though the ending of the chapter is left unclear to where exactly Esau "goes," it is possible (though admittedly questionable) that the narrator is alluding to this "woman taming wild man" motif.

Regarding Gen 25:29, the nature of the "stew" Jacob is cooking is also left vague. Clearly, Esau mistakes it as "red stuff," and the humor used in depicting his character is typical of trickster tales and satire.[48] This type of ambiguity is indicative of trickster tales and they "position readers in relation to the difference of the text by confronting readers with their own potential for misunderstanding even when while compelling participation in the act of creating meaning from shifting texts."[49]

The repetition of Esau's using האדם האדם, characterizing him as "bumbling" and unaccustomed to human social interaction, might also indicate that the stew was a deep red. The word אדם could also possibly be a word play on דם, the Hebrew word for blood. Nahum Sarna notes that "blood was considered to constitute the life essence—and was widely believed to contain magical properties, and it was the symbol of strength and vitality, making the suggestion that [Esau] thinks the soup to be a "blood broth" plausible."[50]

45. King and Stager, *Life in Biblical Israel*, 50–52.

46. BDB, 609.

47. Mobley, "Wild Man," 222.

48. Bledstein, "Binder, Trickster, Heel, and Hairy-Man"; also, Kugel suggests reading this section as satire in his *How to Read the Bible*, 134–35.

49. Monsma, "Wild Man," 84.

50. Sarna, *Genesis*, 182.

After Esau swears to Jacob the birthright, the deception is uncovered—the soup is really lentil stew. Von Rad adds, "[Perhaps] Esau does not even know what Jacob is preparing; it is possible he never had seen it before . . . [or perhaps] he considered it a "blood soup" and is greatly deceived when he finds it to be only a dish of lentils. Esau's subsequent assertion that he was deceived by Jacob twice (ch. 27:36) supports this interpretation."[51]

The fact that Jacob deceives Isaac twice is not to be overlooked, though he does not dupe him in the same way—the end which justifies the means is the same: securing the birthright. This repetition is characteristic of female narrative structure, as Bledstein writes about folklorist and Genizah scholar S. D. Goitein: "When we read for example the story of Eliezer and Rebekah at the well (Gen 24), it is difficult to shake the impression that we have before us a typical woman's story . . . because the technique of double and triple repetition . . . is characteristic of female narrative structure—as I have found it for example in Yemenite collections."[52]

Similarly featured in women's narrative is that "the woman's character is valued, and a man in authority is vulnerable and devious."[53] In the parallel structure of v. 27, it has been mentioned that Esau is a "skillful hunter, a man of the outdoors" contrasted to Jacob, a "mild man who stayed in camp" (Gen 25:27, JPS). Watson, in his *Classical Hebrew Poetry*, discusses that the differences in parallel structure convey implied information to the audience.[54] Although Esau is explicitly referred to as a man twice, denoting descriptions of how he spends his time (in the field, as a hunter, the typical "Wild Man"), Jacob is spoken about only figuratively. It is true that he is called a איש תם, which literally contains the Hebrew equivalent for "man"; however, it denotes a moral and righteous aspect, specifically also used about Job (1:8; 2:3), and its virtuous implications are discussed in Prov 29:10 and 37:37. The absence of the other reference of "man" (to counteract what is present in Esau's phrase) is simply a gender-neutral active participle, as "one dwelling in tents." Jacob, fulfilling the social role of the female, is valued, and as mentioned before, Esau becomes vulnerable submitting to the domestic sphere. Esau's "devious-

---

51. Von Rad, *Genesis*, 261.
52. Bledstein, "Binder, Trickster, Heel, and Hairy-Man," 290–91.
53. Ibid., 291.
54. Watson, *Classical Hebrew Poetry*, 138.

ness" appears in Gen 25:32, as he does not explicitly promise Jacob the birthright; Jacob does not trust Esau to transfer the birthright until he swears to it (v. 33). Although Jacob's righteousness is stated in v. 27, his/her decision to exploit Esau is not without a shade of moral ambiguity. Kugel notes, that "Even to Jacob's most determined supporters, however, some of his deeds must have seemed questionable. Prominent among these was his treatment of Esau with regard to the sale of his birthright."[55]

This questionable behavior is a prominent feature in trickery stories regarding women. Kathleen Ashley writes: "Whether the woman in question uses deception to achieve goals approved by patriarchy (Rebekah, Tamar, Ruth, Rahab, Jael, Judith) or is depicted as a deceiver whose actions threaten the patriarchal order (Jezebel, Potiphar's wife, Dame Folly), the strategy for effective action most closely associated with women characters in the Hebrew Bible is a morally ambivalent one."[56]

And it so happens, that Jacob functioning as a social female might fall into both categories. As Mosma notes, "The trickster performance does not merely invert momentarily the dominant and the oppressed or the center and the marginal. Rather, it reveals social relations within both the center and the margin."[57] Thus, in attempting to revive the interplay of primary characters as well as pariahs, "Characteristics common to many tricksters—shape-shifting, cross-dressing, disruption, playfulness, and liminality—have proven irresistible to critics and theorists of ethnic literatures looking for indigenous and/or marginalized voices with which to challenge the powerful discourses of mainstream critical theory."[58]

The audience for whom this story was originally intended consisted of a knowledgeable community. They would have applauded Jacob's cleverness and duplicity and laughed when the trickster was able to demonstrate Esau's/Edom's inferiority. They, and later generations, would have recognized the symbolism and puns contained within the tales.[59] The references connecting Jacob to the cult of domesticity (through cooking, dwelling in tents), while playing the role of the trickster to usurp procreative power seems to point towards the audience also understanding

---

55. Kugel, *How to Read the Bible*, 140.
56. Ashley, "Interrogating Biblical Deception and Trickster Theories."
57. Monsma, "Wild Man," 91.
58. Ibid., 83.
59. Matthews and Mimi, "Jacob the Trickster and Heir of the Covenant."

Jacob as fulfilling a female social role. The use of paradigms within this narrative (Rebekah/Birth of a Hero; Esau/Wild Man; Jacob/Trickster) are not meant necessarily to prescribe behavior, but provides a framework for analysis. However, it is interesting that if the Birth of the Hero paradigm is easily identifiable as a paradigm that embodies the "female" and the "Wild Man" tradition easily is identifiable as a "male," the use of Jacob as a trickster balances both extremes—by slipping in and out of the female/male realms. It is perhaps difficult to understand a multilayered approach, as it would be easier to adopt a binary outlook that attributes Jacob as "good," Esau as "bad," Jacob as "Israel" or Esau as "Edom/Rome." However, the ambiguity inherent in the narrative is not without intention—expanding from unspoken commentary, "fraught with background" about moral ambiguity, and even gender ambiguity. This narrative, then, agrees with Ackerman's description of the Hebrew Bible; it records both "the mythologies and the histories of both images and lives of the women of ancient Israel. 'It is, if anything, a book not of "either/or" but of "both/and," a book that both glorifies the deeds of men and embraces the tales of women.'"[60]

---

60. Fuchs, "Feminist Approaches to the Hebrew Bible," 89–90, quoting Susan Ackerman, *Warrior, Dancer, Seductress, Queen*, 202.

BIBLIOGRAPHY

Ackerman, Susan. *Warrior, Dancer, Seductress, Queen: Women in Judges and Biblical Israel.* Anchor Bible Reference Library. New York: Doubleday, 1998.

Alter, Robert. *The Art of Biblical Narrative.* New York: Basic Books, 1981.

———. *Genesis.* New York: Norton, 1996.

Ashley, Kathleen. "Interrogating Biblical Deception and Trickster Theories: Narratives of Patriarchy or Possibility?" *Semeia* 42 (1998) 103–11.

Auerbach, Erich. *Mimesis: The Representation of Reality in Western Literature.* Translated by William R. Trask. Princeton: Princeton University Press, 1953.

Bledstein, Adrien Janis. "Binder, Trickster, Heel, and Hairy-Man: Rereading Genesis 27 as a Trickster Tale Told by a Woman." In *A Feminist Companion to Genesis*, edited by Athalya Brenner, 282–95. Sheffield: Sheffield Academic Press, 1993.

Brenner, Athalya. "Female Social Behaviour: Two Descriptive Patterns Within the 'Birth of the Hero' Paradigm." *Vetus Testamentum* 36 (1986) 257–73.

Brown, Francis, S. R. Driver, and Charles A. Briggs. *The Brown-Driver-Briggs Hebrew and English Lexicon.* Peabody, MA: Hendrickson, 2004.

Breyfogle, Caroline M. "The Social Status of Woman in the Old Testament." *Biblical World* 35 (1910) 106–16.

Clines, David J. A. *Interested Parties: The Ideology of Writers and Readers of the Hebrew Bible.* JSOTSS 205; Gender, Culture, Theory 1. Sheffield: Sheffield Academic, 1995.

Chodorow, Nancy. "Gender as a Personal and Cultural Construction." *Signs* 20 (1995) 516–54.

Collins, John, J. *A Short Introduction to the Hebrew Bible.* Minneapolis: Fortress, 2007.

Fuchs, Esther. "Feminist Approaches to the Hebrew Bible." In *The Hebrew Bible: New Insights and Scholarship*, edited by Frederick E. Greenspahn, 76–95. New York: New York University Press, 2008.

Grottanelli, Cristiano. "Tricksters, Scape-Goats, Champions, Saviors." *History of Religions* 23 (1983) 117–39.

Hendel, Ronald S. *The Epic of the Patriarch: The Jacob Cycle and the Narrative Traditions of Canaan and Israel.* Harvard Semitic Monographs 42. Decatur, GA: Scholars, 1987.

King, Philip J., and Lawrence E. Stager. *Life in Biblical Israel.* Louisville: Westminster John Knox, 2001.

Jackson, Melissa. "Lot's Daughters and Tamar as Tricksters." *Journal for the Study of the Old Testament* 98 (2002) 29–46.

King, Philip J., and Lawrence E. Stager. *Life in Biblical Israel.* Library of Ancient Israel. Louisville: Westminster John Knox, 2001.

Kugel, James. *How to Read the Bible: A Guide to Scripture Then and Now.* New York: Free Press, 2007.

Matthews, Victor H., and Frances Mimi, "Jacob the Trickster and Heir of the Covenant: A Literary Interpretation." *Perspectives in Religious Studies* 2 (1985) 185–95.

Meyers, Carol L. "Procreation, Production, and Protection: Male-Female Balance in Early Israel." *Journal of the American Academy of Religion* 51 (1983) 569–93.

Mills, Margaret A. "The Gender of the Trick: Female Tricksters and Male Narrators." *Asian Folklore Studies* 60 (2001) 237–58.

Mobley, Gregory. "The Wild Man in the Bible and the Ancient Near East." *Journal of Biblical Literature* 116 (1997) 217–33.

Monsma, Bradley John. "Active Readers . . . Obverse Tricksters: Trickster Texts and Cross-Cultural Reading." *Modern Language Studies* 26.4 (1996) 83–98.

Newsom, Carol A., and Sharon H. Ringe, editors. *Women's Bible Commentary*. Louisville: Westminster John Knox, 1998.

Niditch, Susan. "Samson as a Culture Hero, Trickster, and Bandit: The Empowerment of the Weak." *Catholic Biblical Quarterly* 52 (1990) 608–25.

———. *Underdogs and Tricksters: A Prelude to Biblical Folklore*. San Francisco: Harper & Row, 1987.

Rad, Gerhard von. *Genesis*. Translated by John H. Marks. Old Testament Library. Philadelphia: Westminster, 1961.

Sarna, Nahum. *Genesis*. The JPS Torah Commentary 1. Philadelphia: The Jewish Publication Society, 1989.

Seeman, Don. "'Where Is Sarah Your Wife?' Cultural Poetics of Gender and Nationhood in the Hebrew Bible." *Harvard Theological Review* 91 (1998) 103–25.

Smith, S. H. "'Heel' and 'Thigh': The Concept of Sexuality in the Jacob-Esau Narratives." *Vetus Testamentum* 40 (1990) 464–73.

Speiser, E. A., trans. *Genesis*. Anchor Bible 1. Garden City, NY: Doubleday, 1962.

Trible, Phyllis. "Depatriarchalizing in Biblical Interpretation." *Journal of the American Academy of Religion* 41 (1973) 30–48.

Watson, Wilfred G. E. *Classical Hebrew Poetry*. JSOTSS 26. Sheffield: JSOT Press, 1984.

5

Of Donkeys and Witnesses

Interpolation or Interpretation?

Giovanna Raengo Czander

THE LAWS IN EXODUS 23:1-9

WHILE WORKING ON THE laws of testimony in Exodus,[1] I came upon two verses which seemed out of place: Exod 23:4-5.[2] The present arrangement of these verses is puzzling, first of all because their content does not seem consistent with the content of the surrounding laws. Exod 23:1-9 begins with laws related to testimony: "You shall not raise a false report, nor shall you join hands with the wicked . . ." and so on. Then the flow of rules about testimony is interrupted in vv. 4 and 5, which deal

---

1. The laws of testimony are conceptually part of the wider topic of evidence. They appear in all the main law collections in the Torah. The commands that directly address the laws of testimony are found in the Book of the Covenant (Exod 20:16; 23:1-3, 6-9), in the Deuteronomic Code (Deut 17:6-7; 19:15-19), and in the Priestly Code (Lev 5:20-26; Num 35:30). Other laws less specifically concerning testimony are found in the Priestly Code (Lev 5:1; Num 5:11-31), in the Holiness Code (Lev 19:15-18; 19:12), and in the Deuteronomic Code (Deut 10:20). The laws of testimony in the Torah address topics such as: false witness (Exod 23:1, 7; Lev 5:20-26; Exod 20:16; Deut 5:20), false accusation (Exod 23:1; Deut 17:6, 7; 19:16; 22:13-21; 20:16; Exod 5:20), obligation to testify (Lev 5:1), absence of witnesses (Exod 23:7, 9; 22:10; Num 5:13; Deut 21:1-9), penalty for refusing to testify (Lev 5:1), and the requirement of a sufficient number of witnesses for capital conviction (Deut 19:15-16; 17:6; Num 35:30).

2. For the history of interpretation of this passage, see Cooper, "Plain Sense of Exodus 23:5."

with property laws, and then it resumes at v. 6 until v. 9. Hence, from the viewpoint of the content, vv. 4 and 5 seem completely unrelated to the surrounding text. Furthermore, vv. 4 and 5 are formulated in a different style compared with the immediately adjacent laws. They are expressed in casuistic form,[3] both beginning with כי. Because of their differences in content and style, these two verses have been considered an interpolation or a later addition, taken from a different source.[4]

The argument I would like to put forth in this article is that Exod 23:4–5, the "laws on donkeys," so to speak, were not casually juxtaposed but purposely combined with the laws of testimony as an interpretation, an expansion, and even a subversion of the concept of *witness* presented in the surrounding laws of testimony. In other words, the present arrangement of these laws has a *rhetorical effect*, and teaches the addressees something *about testimony*.

In order to contextualize this argument, some background about the nature of biblical law is needed.[5] In the last several decades, the idea that biblical laws reflected actual judicial practice in ancient Israel has been questioned in the scholarly field. The assumption that biblical law may not have been practiced emerged as a consequence of Assyriologists questioning the judicial application of the law code *par excellence*, the Code of Hammurabi.[6] While the claim that biblical law was actually applied, at

---

3. I am referring here to the well-known distinction proposed by Alt, between laws expressed apodictic form (beginning with "You shall/you shall not) and casuistic form (beginning with hypothetical cases, such as "if a man..." See Alt, "The Origin of Israelite Law."

4. Wellhausen, *Die Composition des Hexateuchs und der historischen Bücher des Altes Testaments*, 92. More supporters of the claim of vv. 4–5 as interpolated verses are mentioned by Cooper, "Plain Sense," 2 n. 5.

5. A recent article on the state of the question is offered by Wells, "What is Biblical Law?" A good discussion of scholarly positions on the nature of biblical law can be found in Fitzpatrick-McKinley, *The Transformation of Torah from Scribal Advice to Law*.

6. The legal nature of the "Code" of Hammurabi and, by extension, of ancient Near Eastern law has been questioned in 1982 by Jean Bottéro, a French Assyriologist, in an article titled "Is the 'Code' of Hammurabi Really a 'Code'?" See Bottéro, "The 'Code' of Hammurabi," and other essays collected in *Mesopotamia: Writing, Reasoning, and the Gods*. Since then, terms such as code and "collection" are not used consistently in the field. The term "code" is controversial because it alludes to a code of laws that were practiced. Some prefer to use "collection" (see Barmash, *Homicide in the Biblical World*, 6–7). In some cases, they are used interchangeably, but in my opinion the category "collections" is more comprehensive than "codes," since there are collections of law (such as those used for scribal exercises) whose genre is very different from the literary genre named

least to a certain extent, is still held,[7] a number of studies, with whom I agree, have stressed the fact that biblical laws in their present context have primarily a *rhetorical purpose*.[8] To be more precise, I would say that, while it might be difficult to establish the actual purpose of an ancient text, the *effect* produced is certainly rhetorical. Since the argument on the nature of biblical law is difficult to adjudicate, due to the paucity of extra-biblical documents of ancient Israel's actual legal practice, attention has been devoted to biblical law's closest parallels: ancient Near Eastern law codes.[9] The study of these codes suggests that their primary purpose was not judicial application. Various hypotheses have been suggested concerning their purpose: imperial propaganda, theological justification of the ruler, arrangement of scientific knowledge, scribal and wisdom treatises.[10] While there is no consensus on the nature and purpose of ancient Near Eastern (ANE) law codes in the scholarly world, most recognize that the purpose of ANE law codes cannot be limited to their judicial application, though some laws may have been connected to actual legal practice.

A comparison between biblical law and ANE law codes shows that the rhetorical effect of biblical law is produced also by their form. A major difference between ANE law codes and biblical law is the fact that biblical laws are very frequently addressed to a "you," in the second singular or plural person, while this type of address is rarely found in ANE laws.[11]

"law code," and other law collections that have been assembled by scholars. A recent translation of law codes and collections has been done by Roth, *Law Collections from Mesopotamia and Asia Minor*. See also the 2 volumes edited by Westbrook, *A History of Ancient Near Eastern Law*.

7. Wells, *What Is Biblical Law?* identifies four scholarly positions vis-à-vis the question whether biblical law was practiced: a) biblical law as authoritative; b) "Competing sets of authoritative laws"; c) law codes as "theoretical treatises"; d) law codes as "legally descriptive treatises."

8. Patrick, *Old Testament Law*; Patrick, "Studying Biblical Law as a Humanities"; Watts, *Reading Law*.

9. The ANE law codes are: the Laws of Ur-Namma, the Laws of Lipit-Ishtar, the Laws of Eshnunna, the Laws of Hammurabi, the Hittite Laws, the Middle Assyrian Laws, and the Neo-Babylonian Laws. They are frequently compared to the two codes in the Bible: the Covenant Code in Exodus 21–23 and the Deuteronomic Code in Deuteronomy 12–26.

10. See Fitzpatrick-McKinley, *The Transformation of Law from Scribal Advice to Law*.

11. The singular and plural address in the laws is discussed by Weinfeld, *Deuteronomy 1–11*, 15–16.

In light of this second person address, some have concluded that the peculiar form of biblical law has a *rhetorical and pedagogical purpose*.[12] The laws, therefore, have the effect of convincing or instructing (hence the word "*Torah*," instruction) and ultimately, I claim, affecting the identity of the addressees. The laws of testimony occupy a peculiar position within biblical law because they were probably applied in real practice, to a certain extent; yet they retain a meaning and effects that go beyond their judicial application.

The approach to the text adopted in this article presupposes a canonical view of the text. While recognizing that the text has developed over time and has been compiled at different stages by different hands, the emphasis in this article is the text in its final form. Rather than approaching Exod 23:1–9 in light of the history of its composition, and trying to identify the possible historical and literary layers that make up the text in its present shape, I try to make sense of the present shape of the text and of its effects.

Considered in its present form, Exod 23:1–7 seems to be arranged as a chiasm, but is it so? The claim that Exod 23:1–7 is arranged according to a chiastic structure was first put forth by J. W. Welch, later elaborated by D. P. Wright and further discussed by Bernard Jackson.[13] In the following section, Jackson's elaboration of the chiastic structure of the passage identified by Welch and later repurposed by Wright will be discussed and their claim that Exod 23:1–7 is arranged chiastically will be evaluated.

THE CHIASTIC STRUCTURE OF EXODUS 23:1–7

According to Jackson's chiastic arrangement of Exod 23:1–7, the "outer layer" or "envelope" is formed by laws of testimony that surround two casuistic laws at the center of the structure (vv. 4 and 5). The analysis of respectively the laws of testimony and the casuistic laws "on donkeys and enemies" indicates also that the terminology used in this passage is technical legal language.

The passage, as reported by Jackson, is arranged as follows: [14]

---

12. Patrick and Watts emphasize the rhetorical function effects of biblical law.

13. Jackson, *Wisdom-Laws: A Study of the* Mishpatim, 405, follows the chiastic structure of the passage identified by Welch ("Chiasmus in Biblical Law," and elaborated by Wright ("Fallacies of Chiasmus").

14. Jackson, *Wisdom-Laws*, 405.

a) 23:1–2 You shall not (לא) raise a false report (שמע שוא); you shall not join the wicked (רשע)– you shall not (לא) join the majority, thus becoming a false witness (עד חמס)

   b) 23:2–3 You shall not (לא) pervert justice (נטה צדקה), not even to help someone who is poor[15] (ודל) in his suit (בריבו)

      c) 23:4 If you see *your* enemy's (איבך) stranded donkey (or other animal), bring it back to its owner

      c') 23:5 If you see your enemy's (שונאך) donkey lying down, help him out

   b') 23:6 You shall not pervert (נטה, lit. turn aside) the trial of *your* poor person (אביונך) in his suit (בריבו)

a') 23:7 From a false statement (דבר שקר) stay away; do not (לא) slaughter, slay[16] (חרג) the innocent and the just. For I will not acquit (אצדיק) the wicked (רשע).

The text (not included in the chiasm by Welch, Wright, and Jackson) continues with the following provisions:

[23:8 As for a bribe (שחד), you shall not accept it, for a bribe blinds the open-eyed, and subverts the words of the just (דברי צדיקם)

23:9 Even a stranger (וגר), you shall not oppress, for you know the state of mind (נפש) of a stranger, since you were strangers in the land of Egypt].[17]

On the basis of the structure and terminology used throughout the passage as a unit, I argue that all of these laws, including vv. 4–5, are ultimately about what is required of a witness. First, however, a brief clas-

---

15. This instruction must have puzzled even the ancient scribes. Infact, the word ודל has been emended to גדל as in Lev 19:15, assuming that the tendency would be to favor "an important person" in the lawsuit, rather than a poor person. However, if the MT reading is maintained, the message about the laws of testimony changes.

16. The overtones are brutal and violent killing; "implying ruthless violence, esp. private violence; of God slaying in judgment (Gen 20:4; Exod 4:23; 13:15; 22:23; Amos 2:3; 4:10; Lam 2:4, 21; 3:43; Pss 59:12; 78:31, 34; 135:10; 136:18; Num 11:15; 22:33); rarely of judicial killing by men (at God's command), Exod 32:27; Lev 20:15, 16; Num 25:25; Deut 13:10.

17. Vv. 8 and 9 are added here, as will be argued later, because of they are connected with the preceding verses.

sification of witnesses, based upon their functions, is in order.[18] There are two main types of witnesses: observing witnesses and testifying witnesses. *Observing witnesses* can be casual observers of a crime (either eyewitnesses or hearsay witnesses), transaction observers (when they are present at the stipulation of an agreement, for example) or trial observers (they are present during a trial). Observing witnesses can become *testifying witnesses* if they are called to testify in a suit. In ANE law codes and in the Hebrew Bible, testifying witnesses include also accusing parties. This classification clarifies that the laws in Exod 23:1–9 concern different types of witnesses.

LAWS OF TESTIMONY IN EXODUS 23:1–3, 6–7

Exod 23:1–3 combines two laws: the first one forbids the addressee ("you," masculine singular) from repeating in court something that was heard, or overheard, but is not accurate, is "empty" or "false" (שמע שוא) (23:1). The addressee here is therefore a hearsay witness. A similar statement is mirrored in 23:7: "Keep away from a false word (מדבר שקר)" which, in this context, means "false statement, accusation, charge, testimony" and which, therefore, is a little more general than the term "false report" (שמע שוא) in v. 1. The use of שקר and שוא as synonyms in the two versions of the Decalogue, Deut 5:20 and Exod 20:16, suggests that דבר שקר is a technical term indicating "false testimony."

The second law forbids the addressee (same as above) from joining the "wicked" (רשע), or the "many" witnesses (רבים). The results of such action are similar: "becoming a witness of violence" (23:1b) and "transgressing" (23:2b). A "witness of violence" or "violent witness" is more clearly defined in v. 7, which describes the consequences of a "violent witness": "you shall not murder (חרג) the innocent and the just." Therefore, the witness is called "violent" because the consequences of his false testimony are violent, leading to the death of the accused. However, v. 7b, "I will not acquit the רשע" clarifies that in a legal context, this word is more accurately translated as "guilty" or "criminal."[19] The principle implied in this

---

18. Classification proposed by Wells, *Law of Testimony in the Pentateuchal Codes*. I here adopt his terminology.

19. For the meaning of צדק and רשע in a judicial context see also Deut 25:1, which describes a *rib* between two parties and the role of the court. "If there is a dispute between men and they come into court, and the judges decide between them, acquitting the innocent (את־הצדיק הצדקו) and condemning the guilty/criminal (את־הרשע הרשיעו) . . ."

law is that two or more witnesses are sufficient to convict an individual of a capital crime (see the more explicit law in Deut 19:15).[20]

Exodus 23:8–9, as will be argued later, should be considered part of this passage, since they are also connected to it by a syntactic structure similar to v. 3, with the proposed topic at the beginning of the sentence: "as for a poor person, you shall not . . ." (v. 3); "as for a bribe, you shall not . . ." (v. 8); "as for a foreigner, you shall not . . ." (v. 9).

LAWS ON "ENEMIES' DONKEYS" IN EXODUS 23:4–5

At the center of the chiasm lie two casuistic laws. Both are very similar in form and related in content. The first law, in Exod 23:4, is addressed to a "you" (singular): "If you come upon the ox of your enemy (איבך) or his donkey wondering about, you shall certainly return it to him." Who is the "enemy"? In a legal context, the word indicates an adversary, someone who has a pending litigation against the addressee or is ready to take him to court.[21]

The verb פגע, to fall upon, to stumble into, to find, has a different nuance than the verb מצא, to find. The first indicates finding by sheer chance, while the second implies intentionality, finding as a result of searching, with a nuance of purpose rather than chance. Along with its parallel in the following verse, פגע clarifies the identity of the addressee. Who is the "you" addressed in the law? From the formulation of the law itself it appears clear that the addressee is an *eyewitness* (possibly a *casual observer*),[22] someone who "comes upon" a straying animal. The owner of the animal is obviously known to the addressee, as his very own adversary. In light of both these circumstances, the addressee could be tempted to *keep* the animal and later lie about it, as the law in Lev 5:21–22 seems to suggest: "If someone sins and commits faithlessness toward YHWH by lying to another about deposited, entrusted, or stolen property, by extorting another, or by *finding a lost item and lying about it*, and then swears falsely

---

20. Laws related specifically to the sufficient numbers of witnesses are Num 35:30; Deut 17:19; Deut 19:15–20.

21. Argued by Barbiero, *L'asino del nemico*, 75.

22. This meaning is supported also by the parallel use of "If you see . . ." in v. 5. See further.

(וְנִשְׁבַּע עַל־שֶׁקֶר) concerning any of these situations in which someone might act sinfully..."[23]

There is also another danger in this situation, in addition to the temptation to keep the animal. If the person who finds the animal takes it with the intention to return it to its rightful owner, the owner, who happens to be his adversary, and therefore ill-disposed toward him, could take advantage of the situation and accuse him of trying to *steal* the animal. The finder of the animal (an individual, as indicated by his being addressed in the singular) has no witnesses who could support his version of the events; therefore he is in real danger of becoming the victim of a false accusation.[24] This is not a far-fetched scenario, as attested by ANE parallels depicting a similar situation. ANE laws entertain the possibility that the original owner might accuse the individual who takes the roaming animal of stealing it, and hence, if there are no other witnesses present, requires that the individual who takes the roaming animal take an oath to clear himself of the accusation.[25] Returning a straying animal to one's own adversary, therefore, can turn out to be a dangerous enterprise for the person who returns it.

Exodus 23:5, the second law at the center of the chiasm, presents some textual difficulties.[26] The main issues are connected to the meaning of the words שֹׂנַאֲךָ literally, "the one who hates you," רֹבֵץ, "lying down," and

---

23. Wells, *Law of Testimony*, 138–40.

24. See rabbinic sources, cited in Cooper, "Plain Sense."

25. The ANE parallels suggested by Cooper, "Plain Sense," 14 are: LE 50; LH 9–13; MAL C 6; HL 45, 71, 79, 86, also Albeck, "Lost Property." LH 45 (tr. Roth): "If anyone finds implements or an ox, a sheep, a horse, or an ass, he shall drive it back to his owner, and the owner will lead it away. But if he cannot find its owner, he shall secure witnesses (that he is only maintaining custody). Afterwards when its owner finds it, he shall carry off in full what was lost. But if he does not secure witnesses, and afterwards its owner finds it (in his possession), he shall be considered a thief, and he shall make threefold compensation." According to this rule, a person who does not return the animals found can be accused of theft, which is dealt with more directly in LH 70: "If anyone steals an ox, a horse, a mule, or an ass, when its owner claims it, [he shall take] it in full. In addition the thief shall give to him double. He shall look to his house for it." HL 75: "If anyone hitches up an ox, a horse, a mule or an ass, and it dies, [or] a wolf devours [it], or it gets lost, he shall give it in full. But if he says: 'It died by the hand of a god,' he shall take an oath to that effect." This rule illustrates some of the dangers connected with keeping something in custody. The person responsible for safekeeping other people's goods is held accountable for possible *damage* to those goods. For example, "If an ox is found dead on someone's property, the property-owner shall give 2 oxen. He shall look to his house for it" (HL 72).

26. Childs, *Exodus*, 450.

the whole second part of the verse which plays on the verb עזב, "to abandon," by extension, to relieve. רבץ does not necessarily imply that the animal is "struggling" under the burden, as thought of in rabbinic literature, since in most occurrences it means simply "lying down,"[27] even "resting" (often used of animals).[28] The other instance in which the verb רבץ is used referring to a donkey is found in Num 22:27. When Balaam's donkey sees the angel of the Lord and ותרבץ תחת בלעם, he "*lies down* under Balaam," this does not necessarily imply that the animal is struggling, nor that he is peacefully resting. Rather, the verb indicates that the donkey (out of fear, from the context) does not want to co-operate, as Balaam's reaction confirms (Balaam becomes enraged and hits the animal with his stick). The picture we have here in Exodus 23, then, is that of an animal who is loaded and, maybe, but not necessarily, because of it, does not intend to co-operate with his owner, who is present (עמו).

The root חדל in a legal context means abstaining from performing a required duty, such as observing Passover (Num 9:13) or making a vow (Deut 23:23), both followed by ל.[29]

The real interpretive *crux* in this verse is the verb עזב, to forsake, or, only in this unique case, to free someone. The textual variants in the Syriac, the LXX, and the Vulgate attest to the long-standing difficulty of the text. There are several possible translations, some of which are here indicated, that can be completely contradictory:

1. If you witness the donkey of your adversary lying down under his burden, would you leave him to it (i.e., the burden)? You should free him (i.e., the donkey) with him (i.e., the owner), or in his [owner's] presence.

2. If you observe the donkey of your adversary lying down under his burden and you forbear abandoning him to it, you shall certainly abandon (i.e., the donkey) with it (the burden).

---

27. See Isa 11:7.

28. Cooper and others show that רבץ means "lying down" and does not imply that the animal is overloaded or struggling. Cooper, "Plain Meaning," 3.

29. Both instances (Num 9:13 and Deut 23:23) are followed by ל + infinitive. Exod 23:5 חדל is followed by מן.

3. If you observe . . . should you desist from abandoning him? You should certainly abandon (the donkey) with him (the owner, who is present).[30]

The beginning of Exod 23:5, "if you see . . . (כי תראה)" addresses the "you" (singular) as a potential *observing witness*, someone who "sees." In this context of norms related to testimony, the verb "to see" is used in a technical sense, so much that it could be translated as: "if you witness your adversary's donkey . . ." Seeing is intrinsically connected with witnessing. Lev 5:1 gives the closest we can find to a definition of witness: "someone who sees or knows." That seeing is one of the main activities of a witness is also confirmed by Exod 22:9: אין ראה, if there is no "seer" or no-one "seeing," which means "if there is no witness" (in this specific case a *transaction witness* who can testify that one individual has given his good to another individual for safekeeping). That this instruction refers to a witness is also confirmed by the fact that an oath is required to adjudicate the dispute (a requirement when there are no witnesses, known both in the Hebrew Bible and throughout ANE law codes).[31]

"Seeing" is a typical action pertaining to witnesses. In fact, it is not limited to eyesight. In Exod 20:22, YHWH tells the Israelites, "You have *seen* that from the mountain I have *spoken* with you." On the mountain, where the theophany had taken place, there had been both visual and audible signs of YHWH's presence and handing of the law. The verb ראה here encompasses both seeing and hearing. Furthermore, it has legal overtones, that is, it reminds the addressee-Israel that seeing implies the legal responsibility of being ready to testify in the future about what was seen and heard. In brief, "seeing" in a legal context, automatically turns the "seer" into an "observing witness."

The verb חדל generally means to cease; in the laws, see Num 9:13 (neglecting to celebrate the Sabbath). Here it is followed by מן, which in Deut 15:11 means to cease + vb. In Deut 23:23 again it has the meaning of forbearing a legal duty, "if you forbear to fulfill your vows, it is not a sin." The translation, therefore, would be as follows: "When/if you witness the

---

30. For a full discussion of the possible emendations and translations, see Cooper, "Plain Sense," esp. 12–18.

31. See Losier, "Witness in Israel of the Hebrew Scriptures in the Context of the Ancient Near East"; and Tikva Frymer-Kensky, "Judicial Ordeal in the Ancient Near East."

donkey of your adversary lying down under his weight and you neglect relieving him: you should certainly help/deliver (=unload) *with* him/in his (i.e., the enemy's) presence."

While the idea of a chiastic arrangement of Exod 23:1–7 is certainly appealing and has found a certain success in the field, there is a problem. This chiasm is not perfect, for two reasons. First, in order to achieve a perfect chiastic structure, Welch and Wright leave out vv. 8 and 9, which are closely related, from the viewpoint of the content, to the previous verses. If considered as a whole, Exod 23:1–9 has a structure that has some resemblance to a chiasm but is more unbalanced, as the second half (vv. 5–9) is longer than the first half (vv. 1–4).[32] Secondly, the second half of the quasi-"chiasm" is enriched by several *motive clauses*, such as: "for (כי) I will not acquit the innocent" (v. 7b), "for (כי) a bribe blinds . . ." (v. 8), and the double motive clause in v. 9: "you know the נפש of a stranger, for (כי) you yourselves were strangers in the land of Egypt." This abundance of motive clauses contributes to a further imbalance in the chiastic arrangement of the passage.

In spite of its imperfections as a chiasm, the arrangement of the passage can hardly be coincidental. Furthermore, it shows a certain unity, both from the viewpoint of the terminology, the arrangement and, as will be illustrated shortly, the content. There are too many repetitions and connections among the different elements of this "chiasm" to justify the idea of an interpolation or misplacement of vv. 4 and 5. Though not a perfect chiasm, this arrangement *shows purpose*. Although there is no apparent connection between the laws of testimony and the laws on donkeys, the text shows not a simple juxtaposition of the two sets of laws, but a real attempt at combining them. Maybe chiasm is not the exact pattern that underlies this passage, but the numerous repetitions and the arrangement, as will be illustrate shortly, show that it was done purposely.

IMPLICATIONS OF THE PRESENT ARRANGEMENT OF THE TEXT

Why was the text given its present arrangement? While Welch, Wright, and Jackson have not explored the implications of the chiastic structure they proposed, it seems undeniable that the first conclusion that can be

---

32. Jackson, *Wisdom-Laws*, 405 n. 86, is willing to include v. 8, but does not mention v. 9.

drawn from the existence of a quasi-chiastic structure is that it shows a *purpose* in the compilation of the passage. In other words, the discovery of a quasi-chiastic structure does not exclude that the two casuistic verses (4–5) were inserted at a different time and from a different "legal" source. However, it shows that this insertion was done with intention. The redactor of the text arranged these laws so that they would be read in light of each other. I would like to argue that all of the laws established in this passage tell us something about *testimony*.

First of all, the intercalation of instructions on false witness and the prohibition against showing partiality toward certain categories of people (such as the poor, the innocent, the foreigner) indicate the absolute *priority and unbendability* of the rules on false testimony. Even though these categories have a special status in the eyes of the legislator elsewhere in the Torah (see, for example, Lev 19:15), their status does not constitute grounds for an exception to the rules on false testimony. In other words, the categories or people here mentioned—the poor, the enemy, the one who hates you, the innocent, the just, could all be the subject of a possible exception to the laws of testimony. Can that law be bent for a poor person? In the case of an enemy? What about a just person or an innocent person? Can false witness be given to protect an innocent or a just person? The rule in v. 6, "you shall not deviate a trial/justice of your poor in his suit" makes clear that there are no exceptions to the laws of testimony. The logic underlying the flow of the laws in Exod 23:1–9 supports my claim that the main idea of this quasi-chiastically arranged text is testimony. The arrangement flows from possible objections that can be raised to the main idea: "You shall not give false witness." Possible objection: "What if there is a significant number of witnesses who accuse the person?" Answer: "You shall not join hands with false witnesses … You shall not join the majority (רבים) …" (v. 2). Another objection to the general rule could be raised: "What if the accused is a poor person, who could benefit from a false witness? Can false witness be given to help a poor person in his suit?" The laws of testimony, however, do not allow for any exception, not even to help someone who is poor. "Even a poor person (דל) you shall not favor" is the answer (in v. 3 and the corresponding v. 6, which adds "your" poor, making it even more personal for the addressee). The final verses (7–9) answer other possible objections: "What if I find myself involved in a case as witness; would that justify my giving false testimony?" "What if I am offered a bribe?" "What if the suit is against a foreigner, one who is not my kinsman (whom I would be obliged to help)?"[33] The point again seems to be clear: there are no exceptions to the rule prohibiting false witness.

The two rules concerning the "enemy" or, as previously argued, the "legal adversary" in vv. 4 and 5 allude to legal implications connected to testimony and imply a *risk* for the individual who puts these rules into practice. The first verse (Exod 23:4), which considers the case of a wandering animal, could give the opportunity to bear false witness or false accusation. How? According to Exod 22:4, if an animal is found wandering about in someone else's field, it could have been stolen. "If the stolen beast is found alive in his possession, whether it is an ox or an ass or a sheep, he shall pay double."[34] In other words, someone found with an animal that does not belong to him could be accused of having stolen the animal. Incidentally, in the Decalogue, Exod 20:17 prohibits from coveting one's neighbor's house, wife, servants, his ox, donkey or anything else that belongs to one's neighbor. Interestingly, in the Decalogue too, the rule about ox and donkey follows the command forbidding false witness. Even in the event that the Decalogue was in fact composed later than the Covenant Code, the proximity of these two rules is intriguing. Unfortunately, this proximity cannot be pursued in this article. Another issue that cannot be explored in this article is a similar law found in Deut 22:1. This law, however concerns the animal belonging to one's kinsman, רֵעַ: "You shall not see *your kinsman's* ox or his sheep go astray..." In the case of Exod 23, however, the owner *hates* or is *the legal adversary of* the person who found the animal. Therefore, finding a stranded animal and taking it back to the rightful owner could expose the finder to the accusation of theft while in possession of the animal. Since the owner is hostile ("an enemy" or "adversary") to the individual returning the animal, the owner could use this opportunity to accuse this individual of having stolen the animal.

The second instruction (v. 5) too implies a risk, but that risk seems not to be of a legal nature. Given the situation, one with an uncooperative animal and in the owner's presence, a question arises: how would one help a stubborn loaded donkey? Only, it appears, by *taking some of its burden*

---

33. Both versions of the Decalogue command: "You shall not bear false witness against your neighbor."

34. A parallel in Hittite law, n. 45 reads: "If anyone finds implements, [he shall bring] them back to their owner. He (the owner) will reward him. But if the finder does not give them (back), he shall be considered a thief." Trans., Roth, *Law Collection from Mesopotamia and Asia Minor*, 223.

off and carrying it or putting it down. How does that reconcile with the instruction asking to do this for *the one who hates you*? How does this pose a risk to the one who helps? Could taking the load off the donkey expose the helper to being accused of theft (similarly to v. 4)? It seems plausible that a vicious adversary could take the opportunity to accuse the helper of trying to steal part of the משא, the cargo. However, in light of the laws in Exod 22:13–14, it would seem that it is legally less risky to help one's enemy in this circumstance. This rule implies a different kind of risk. Incidentally, Patrick mentions precisely this instruction to support his claim that "the law books were intended not for judicial application but for instruction in the values, principles, concepts, and procedures of the unwritten divine Law."[35] The key to unraveling this verse is the word עמו, "with him [the owner]."[36] This points to a specific situation addressed by the laws of safekeeping and stealing. In case of property damage, the laws make a distinction between a situation in which the owner is present (Exod 22:13) and a case in which the owner is *not* present (Exod 22:14).[37] If the owner is present when a property is damaged, the "keeper" is not responsible, and is not required to give the owner compensation for the damage. In this context, therefore, the word "with him (עמו)" means "in his presence, when he is present." When applied to Exod 23:5, the owner's presence when his donkey is lying down under the weight does not make the addressee liable of being accused of trying to steal either the animal or its cargo.[38] Therefore, the observing witness, who is also the addressee of the law, is invited to help his adversary *beyond the legal requirements* and to go beyond human emotions, such as giving into the temptation to continue on without helping (לו מעזב והדלת).

The two casuistic laws in Exod 23:4–5 are parallel but not repetitive. They are actually in a *crescendo,* and present two slightly different situations. The first one considers a situation in which the owner of the

---

35. Patrick, *Old Testament Law*, 198.

36. עמו can also mean "with it" (i.e., the cargo). In either case, it entails the owner's presence "with the burden."

37. Exodus 22:13–14: "If a man borrows anything of his neighbor, and it is hurt or dies, the owner not being with it (עמו), he shall make full restitution. If the owner was with it (עמו), he shall not make restitution; if it was hired, it came for its hire (or it is reckoned in, comes into, its hire)" (NRV, vv. 14–15).

38. The rule in Deut 22:4 may sound similar, but there are numerous differences: the owner is not present, the animals are wandering about, and no mention is made of any of them carrying a burden. ל + infinitive.

animal is not present. In the second case the owner is present (עמו). So, while in the first case, the addressee of the laws is required to take the wandering animal and return it, in the second case, the presence of the owner could exonerate the addressee from having to help. The effect of the juxtaposition of the two laws is that the first norm is further entwined in the second, where *even if the owner is present,* help is to be provided. This is a kind of help that requires co-operating with the owner himself (עמו intended also more plainly as "together with him") though he is "the one who hates" the addressee, his legal adversary.

WHO ARE THE ADDRESSEES OF THE LAWS IN EXODUS 23:1–9?

Several scholars[39] understand 23:1–3 as addressed to witnesses, and 6–9 to judges, but is it so? Is it necessary to postulate a change of addressees or can witnesses be the addressees throughout the whole passage?[40] On the basis of the terminology used, I argue that all these laws address their audience *as observing witnesses* (who are also potential *testifying witnesses*). One of the key terms in support of this argument is the verb (ראה) in v. 5, "If you see . . ." In this context, this verb does not simply mean "to see." It implies that the person who sees is a (casual) observing witness. It may well be translated: "If you witness your adversary's ox or donkey . . ." The meaning of seeing = witnessing is confirmed in v. 8, "as for a bribe, do not take it, because the bribe *blinds the open-eyed* (יעור פקחים)," that is, the witnesses: both those who might have observed a crime or a transaction and those who are trial observing witnesses or about to testify in a trial. These could be the judges, but why do we need to assume a switch of addressees? It appears that the text here is still addressed to the witnesses. The word that could be used to oppose my hypothesis is (שחד), the bribe used to corrupt judges. At this point, we need to entertain the question: Is שחד only related to judges? *Could this bribe be used also to corrupt witnesses?* From the occurrences of the word, and its parallel כפר, it appears clear that a bribe can be used both to corrupt judges and witnesses

---

39. Childs, *Exodus*, 482; Bovati, *Re-Establishing Justice*, 198; Patrick, *Old Testament Law*, 89–90; Barbiero, *L'asino del nemico*, 27. Not so Cornelis Houtman, *Exodus*, vol. 3, 188–89.

40. Barbiero, *L'asino del nemico*.

alike. As Isaiah says, "*everyone* loves a bribe (שחד)" (Isa 1:23).[41] Though usually שחד indicates a bribe used to corrupt judges, there are texts that suggest that שחד can be used also to corrupt witnesses. Prov 17:23 reads: "A wicked man (רשע) receives a bribe (שחד) from the bosom to pervert the ways of justice." In most cases, רשע is a false witness, not a judge.[42] Another text which shows the term שחד referring to the corruption of witnesses is Psalm 15. A similar text in Deut 16:19, possibly a proverb, further supports the idea that Exod 23:1–9 is addressed to witnesses. "You shall not accept a bribe, for the bribe blinds the eyes of the wise, and perverts the *words* (דברי) of the righteous (צדיקים)."

Here צדיקים, as previously argued, means "truthful witnesses."[43]

CONCLUSIONS

I have argued that the present arrangement of the laws in Exod 23:1–9 is not the result of an interpolation but is purposeful. The two laws about "donkeys" (Exod 23:4–5) intertwined with the laws about "witnesses" (Exod 23:1–3, 6–9) have the effect of giving a broad and challenging concept of witness. In addition to the idea of a witness who does not join the majority to subvert justice, and does not bear false testimony under any circumstances (Exod 23:1–3, 6–9), the two laws on "donkeys" put forth the idea that being a witness is not only about observing and testifying with integrity, but also about "doing," even when "doing" entails a risk and going beyond one's natural tendency to withdraw help from one's adversary.

---

41. The context of Isaiah's passage refers especially to leaders, but the statement is omni-comprehensive, having the flavor of a proverb.

42. Of the texts where the term שחד occurs, the following are not clearly referring to a judge: Deut 10:17; 16:19; 27:25, where taking a bribe is associated to striking someone, an activity which pertains to witnesses, more than judges; 1 Kgs 15:19; 2 Kgs 16:8; Prov 6:35 (parallel with כפר); Isa 5:23; Ezek 22:12. Psalm 26:10 clearly uses שחד referring it to witnesses (אנשי דמים). Ezekiel 22:23 too, in my opinion, refers to witnesses. The text that is most convincingly about witnesses is Psalm 15, where the just/witness is described: "He walks blamelessly, and does what is right, and *speaks the truth from his heart, who does not slander with his tongue*, and does no evil to his friend, . . . and does not take a bribe (שחד) against the innocent." For the use of the term, see also Bovati, *Re-Establishing Justice*, 195.

43. Qoheleth 3:17. Bovati, *Re-Establishing Justice*, 203, shows that צדיק is "a) Someone who claims innocence or b) someone who is (or claims to be) poor, humble and oppressed. The latter case typically represents those who, on account of their own lack of power, are continually victims of the oppression."

In order to build up to this broader idea of "witness," the two casuistic laws in Exod 23:4–5 are arranged in a *crescendo*. As we have seen, the first one considers a situation in which the owner of the animals is not present. In the second case the owner is present (עמו). So, while in the first case, the addressee of the laws is required to take the wandering animal and return it, at his own risk, in the second case, the presence of the owner could exonerate the addressee from having to help. The effect of the juxtaposition of the two laws is that the first norm is further stretched in the second, where *even if the owner is present* or *in spite of the owner's presence* help is to be provided. This is a kind of help that requires co-operating with the owner himself, though he is "the one who hates" the addressee, his legal adversary.

As argued in the article, the use of the verb *to see* (ראה) and of the *second person address*, it was argued, engages the *addressees* of the laws by appealing to them as potential witnesses (both observing and testifying witnesses). Whoever identifies himself or herself with the addressee of these laws is called to a broad understanding of the requirements about being witness. To the "negative" requirements ("you shall not") explicated in the laws about testimony (Exod 23:1–3, 6–9) the laws in Exod 23:4–5 add the obligation for witnesses take a "positive" action. Being an observing witness (one who happens to "see") entails the responsibility of "doing something." The addressee *sees* his enemy in trouble and is obliged to *help* him, even when this is risky or seems to go beyond the call of duty.

In conclusion, the two casuistic laws intentionally intertwined with the laws of testimony in Exod 23:1–9 challenge the addressees to a broad understanding of the concept of witness: testimony is not only about observing and about testifying, but also about having integrity and about "doing," even when doing entails taking a risk and going beyond one's natural tendency to withdraw help from one's enemy. Exodus 23:1–9 is therefore more than laws regulating the behavior of witnesses. It attempts to shape the addressees as witnesses and shows them how they ought to behave. Not just in court, but also in life.

BIBLIOGRAPHY

Albeck, Ahalom. "Lost Property." In *Encyclopaedia Judaica*, 11:504–6. Jerusalem: Keter, 1972.

Alt, Albrecht. "The Origins of Israelite Law." In *Essays on Old Testament History and Religion*, 79–132. Translated by R. A. Wilson; Oxford: Blackwell, 1966. German original 1934.

Barbiero, Gianni. *L'asino del nemico. Rinuncia alla vendetta e amore del nemico nella legislazione dell'Antico Testamento (Es 23, 4–5; Dt 22, 1–4; Lv 19, 17–18)*. Analecta biblica 128. Rome: Pontificio Istituto Biblico, 1991.

Barmash, Pamela. *Homicide in the Biblical World*. Cambridge: Cambridge Univ Press, 2005.

Bottéro, Jean. *Mesopotamia: Writing, Reasoning, and the Gods*. Translated by Bahrani and Van de Mieroop. Chicago: University of Chicago Press, 1992.

Bovati, Enrico. *Re-Establishing Justice: Legal Terms, Concepts and Procedures in the Hebrew Bible*. Translated by M. J. Smith. JSOTSS 105. Sheffield: Sheffield Academic, 1994.

Childs, Brevard S. *The Book of Exodus: A Critical, Theological Commentary*. Old Testament Library. Philadelphia: Westminster, 1974.

Cooper, Alan "The Plain Sense of Exodus 23:5." *Hebrew Union College Annual* 59 (1998) 1–22.

Fitzpatrick-McKinley, Anne, *The Transformation of Torah from Scribal Advice to Law*. JSOTSS 287. Sheffield: Sheffield Academic, 1999.

Frymer-Kensky, Tikva. "The Judicial Ordeal in the Ancient Near East." 2 vols. PhD diss., Yale University, 1977.

Jackson, Bernard S. *Wisdom-Laws: A Study of the Mishpatim of Exodus 21:1—22:16*. Oxford: Oxford University Press, 2006.

Losier, Mary Alma. "Witness in Israel of the Hebrew Scriptures in the Context of the Ancient Near East." PhD diss., University of Notre Dame, 1979.

Patrick, Dale. *Old Testament Law*. Atlanta: John Knox, 1985.

———. "Studying Biblical Law as a Humanities." In *Semeia 45: Thinking Biblical Law*, edited by Dale Patrick, 24–47. Atlanta: Scholars, 1989.

Roth, Martha. *Law Collections from Mesopotamia and Asia Minor*. SBL Writings from the Ancient World Series 6. 2nd ed. Atlanta: Scholars, 1997.

Watts, James W. *Reading Law: The Rhetorical Shape of the Pentateuch*. Biblical Seminar 59. Sheffield: Sheffield Academic, 1999.

Weinfeld, Moshe. *Deuteronomy 1–11*. Anchor Bible 5. New York: Doubleday, 1991.

Welch, J. W. "Chiasmus in Biblical Law." In *Jewish Law Studies IV: The Boston Conference Volume*, edited by B. S. Jackson, 5–22. Atlanta: Scholars, 1990.

Wellhausen, Julius. *Die Composition des Hexateuchs und der historischen Bücher des Altes Testaments*. Berlin: Reimer, 1889.

Wells, Bruce. *The Law of Testimony in the Pentateuchal Codes*. Beihefte zur Zeitschrift für altorientalische und biblische Rechtsgeschichte 4. Wiesbaden: Harrassowitz, 2004.

———. "What is Biblical Law? A Look at Pentateuchal Rules and Near Eastern Practice." *Catholic Biblical Quarterly* 70 (2008) 223–43.

Westbrook, Raymond, editor. *A History of Ancient Near Eastern Law*. Handbook of Oriental Studies. Section 1: The Near and Middle East 72. Leiden: Brill, 2003.

Wright, D. P. "The Fallacies of Chiasmus: A Critique of Structures Proposed for the Covenant Collection (Ex 20:23—23:19)." *Zeitschrift für altorientalische und biblische Rechtsgeschichte* 10 (200) 93–142.

6

The Influence of Egyptian Throne Names on Isaiah 9:5

A Reassessment of the Debate in Light of the Divine Designations in the Book of Isaiah

MÁIRE BYRNE

INTRODUCTION

ISAIAH 9:5[1] HAS GENERATED much debate about every aspect of its significance. There exists a diverse range of theories as to whether it actually speaks of the birth of a child, and if indeed this child is a king or member of a royal family or if the titles are referring to a divine being. Relationships between the royal-sounding titles in the verse and Egyptian throne titles have been proposed by many commentators. Von Rad initially proposed the parallel in 1947, suggesting that the Judaean enthronement ritual was heavily dependent on the corresponding Egyptian ritual.[2] The Egyptian protocol contained the five names of the new pharaoh's titulary and the legitimation of his rule by the deity's acknowledgment of the king as the offspring of the deity. In this case, von Rad argues that Isa 9:5 reflects the king's divine sonship as well as his five-fold royal titulary. This suggests that the speaker of the verse is not the people, but rather the deity.[3] Alt argued that the text of Isa 8:23 to 9:5 was composed for

---

1. This work shall follow the Hebrew numbering of the text. For English translations the verse is numbered 9:6.
2. Von Rad, "Das judäische Königsritual."
3. Ibid., 216.

Hezekiah's enthronement and that it reflected the strong influence of Egyptian enthronement rituals. Verse 5, therefore, did not refer to the actual physical birth of a child, but rather to the legitimation of the new king at his coronation. It would follow that the names are enthronement names parallel to the fivefold titulary of the Egyptian kings.[4] J. J. M. Roberts provides an excellent overview of the current research and debate that stems from this von Rad–Alt consensus.[5]

Christian readings of the verse tend to classify the verse as heralding the birth of Jesus.[6] It is noteworthy that many commentaries on the verse are often caught up in a discussion of the messianic overtones without allowing for any examination of the text itself.[7] When this verse is viewed against the rest of the book of Isaiah there is a stark contrast in the use of the titles. Only one of the titles (Mighty God) is used elsewhere in the sixty-six chapters. Designations, particularly those associated with the divine, tend to be distributed in recognizable patterns throughout the text and respect the traditional divisions of Proto-, Deutero-, and Trito-Isaiah.[8] YHWH is often termed a king in the text, so it is noteworthy that these titles are only used once in another part of the book. The substantial difference in style from the rest of the text would indicate unique outside influence in this verse. With the overall use of titles within the text in mind, the influence of Egyptian throne names on 9:5 is worth revisiting in order to assert to whom the text is referring and if the titles are indeed divine.

EGYPTIAN THRONE NAMES

The actual possession of a name was of vital importance to the ancient Egyptians. A baby was given its name immediately after birth so that it would have a name even if it died. There is a close connection between the power of naming and the element of magic in Egyptian religious thought. Knowledge of a name might have conferred some secret power over that named person, and it followed that to obliterate the name inscribed on a king's cartouche was to jeopardize his continuing existence in the after-

---

4. Alt, "Jesaja 8:23—9:6."
5. Roberts, "Whose Child Is This?"
6. Pentiuc, *Jesus the Messiah in the Hebrew Bible*, 49–50.
7. For several examples, see Sawyer, *The Fifth Gospel*, 1–20, especially 1–3.
8. Byrne, "'My People Shall Know My Name.'"

life.⁹ For such reasons, the naming of the Egyptian kings or pharaohs was a complicated business, normally hedged with precautions. In the early dynasties, the king was given three names. These were later added to as the concept of the god-king developed. By the Ninth Dynasty (beginning in 2160 BCE), the final form was established. The five royal titles consist of four names that the king assumed on the day of his accession, along with a fifth name that had been given to him at birth. Three of the names stress the king's role as god, and two emphasize the perceived division of Egypt into two lands, both under his control.

Examination of the Five Throne Names

The Horus names were the earliest of the names given to the king.¹⁰ They were painted on pottery vessels, palettes, and mace heads; carved in ivory and wooden labels; and often inscribed onto the side of cliffs. The Horus name was always written within a *serekh*, a rectangle, bordered at the bottom by the kind of recessed paneling found on the facades of early mud-brick tombs and palaces and topped by the falcon god, Horus. This represented the belief from the pre-dynastic era that the king was the physical embodiment of Horus on earth. Osiris was believed to have been the king of Egypt before his death and consequently, as his son, Horus had inherited the kingship.

The second of the throne names was called the *nbty* or "two females" name.¹¹ *Nbt* was the Egyptian word for "female" and was pluralized by the addition of the "y." In this case the "Two Females" referred to are the goddesses of Upper and Lower Egypt—the vulture goddess *Nekhbet* of El-Kab in Upper Egypt and the cobra goddess *Wadjet* of Buto in the Delta—two of the most important cities of the pre-dynastic northern and southern chiefdoms.¹² The "Two Females" name of "He who belongs to the two females" placed the king under the direct protection of *Nekhbet* and *Wadjet* and thus represented his close association with both regions of Egypt. It also represented the duality of the geographical balance of the Two Lands in the person of the king. Duality was an all-important concept in the

---

9. Shafer, et al., *Religion in Ancient Egypt*, 59.
10. Shaw, *The Oxford History of Ancient Egypt*, 6.
11. Gardiner, *Egyptian Grammar*, 73.
12. Pinch, *Egyptian Mythology*, 211.

Egyptian worldview; the reconciliation of opposites in order to maintain the established order was a fundamental role of kingship.

The third name was the "Golden Horus" name, and its origins may be traced in royal inscriptions of the First and Third Dynasties[13] and in the Palermo Stone. It was simply written with the hieroglyphic for gold when it was originally introduced, so perhaps it symbolized the divinity of the king, as gold was considered eternal and the gods were said to have skin that was made from gold.[14]

The "prenomen" or throne name was also known as the "Lord of Two Lands" name or the "King of Upper and Lower Egypt," as it later came to be called. This title which literally means "he of the sedge and bee" or dual-aspected king, may have symbolized the dual natures of human and divine that were part of kingship.[15] The sedge plant is the traditional symbol of Upper Egypt and the bee the symbol of Lower Egypt. It was composed at the king's accession to the throne and by the Fourth Dynasty (2613–2494 BCE) invariably incorporated the name of the sun-god, Ra.[16]

The second name, or *nomen*, was the name given at the birth of the king.[17] It was usually preceded by the titles *Sa-Re* or "Lord of Appearances or Crowns," for example the well-known "Ramesses," and sometimes had another epithet added, such as "beloved of Amun" or "divine ruler of Thebes." Modern historians and Egyptologists normally refer to kings or pharaohs by the *nomen* or birth name, distinguishing between kings of the same name by adding a Roman numeral as appropriate.

The Accession of the King in Ancient Egypt

In order to fully comprehend any influence the throne names of ancient Egyptian kings had on the text of Isa 9:5, it is beneficial to investigate the accession rites of ancient Egypt. In general in a monarchical society, the coronation or ascent to the throne by a king is the official act that most clearly demonstrates the sacral character of the kingdom or society. Until the twentieth century, two characteristics in the coronations of kings and emperors still existed: through their ascent to the throne, the monarch

---

13. First Dynasty 3000–2890 BCE and Third Dynasty 2686–2613 BCE.
14. Wilkinson, *Early Dynastic Egypt*, 207.
15. O'Connor and Silverman, *Ancient Egyptian Kingship*, 127.
16. Allen, *Middle Egyptian*, 65.
17. David, *Handbook to Life in Ancient Egypt*, 219.

assumes a position that is higher than that of their subjects. The accession to the throne is connected with supernatural powers, culminating in the beginning of a new era.[18]

The act of adoration of a king is based on the throne rite, which is known only in areas having national kings. Though ascent to the throne and coronation with investiture are universal, there are many other rituals that are often connected with sacred kingship. Among these are the anointment of the kings of Israel, India, and Iran,[19] which was originally a ritual that gave strength to the recipient, as noted in primitive cultures (for example, rubbing with the fat of a lion); pseudo-fights or sham battles, from which the king emerges as victor; and ritual cleansing and meals. The survival of elements of sacred kingship in the Christian West is especially evident in coronation rites.

With this idea of sacred kingship in mind, it is beneficial to examine each designation in 9:5b, firstly in isolation and then viewed in a quartet. In examining each in turn, it is also interesting to briefly survey how commentators have translated and analyzed each term.

TITLES IN ISAIAH 9:5

Wonder Counselor / Marvelous Counselor[20] *(פלא יועץ)*

There are many variations in the translation of this term, probably as a result of a lack of syntactic agreement between the two terms. Delitzsch's assertion that the two terms should be split into "wonder" and "counselor" has since been challenged by the accentuation of the Masoretic text, which would support the combining of the two in one designation.[21] Blenkinsopp defines this designation as "a juxtaposition of two words syntactically unrelated [but which] indicates the capacity to elaborate good plans and stratagems."[22] The author of the biblical text has previously alluded to the fact that YHWH possesses the ability to formulate and carry out effective plans as the Holy One of Israel in 5:19 and "plans of old" brought to fruition in 25:1. Kaiser's translation of the Hebrew as

---

18. Woolley *Coronation Rites*, 1–6.
19. Hastings, et al., *Encyclopedia of Religion and Ethics*, 1:21B.
20. Translation used by Blenkinsopp, *Isaiah 1–39*.
21. Delitzsch, *Biblical Commentary on the Prophecies of Isaiah*. Childs, *Isaiah*, 78, discusses Delitzch's theory.
22. Blenkinsopp, *Isaiah 1–39*, 250.

"he who plans wonders"[23] is in agreement with this image, and he sees the designation as highlighting how the referent will require no external advice for his plans that will be universally carried through. Jenson notes that the designation "signifies not so much that he would in fact counsel others as that he would be able to devise wonderful plans."[24] The designation does appear to pick up on the attributes already expressed regarding a king of the future in 11:2 and indeed later in the text of YHWH in 28:29. De Jonge's suggestion that the terms mean "he who takes decisions based on divine (secret) knowledge"[25] is perhaps allowing an air of mystery that belies the practical nature of the terminology. The designation depicts the referent as one who can take control of any situation with a well formulated plan of action. Those who allow this "wonder counselor" to take the lead will see the plans carried through to completion. They do not need to concern themselves with how the plans were enacted or indeed formulated, rather they should be safe in the knowledge that the skills possessed by this "mighty planner" will result in "wonderful" results, whether in the earthly or divine realms.

Mighty God / Warrior God (אל גבור)

The question of the relationship between the biblical use of אל and the Semitic concepts of *El* has received much attention particularly since the discovery of the Ugaritic texts, which have apparently established the fact that the term *El* was used in reference to a personal god and not merely as a generic term in the ancient Semitic world. It is also the most widely distributed name among Semitic-speaking peoples for the deity, occurring in some form in every Semitic language except Ethiopic. Pope, in his study of the term in the Ugaritic, notes that it is the most frequently occurring proper name for the deity throughout the ancient Semitic world.[26] It is found throughout the Hebrew Bible, but most frequently in the book of Job and the book of Psalms. The etymology of the word is obscure.[27] The same variety of derivations is attributed to this term as to אלהים, the most probable of which is Hebrew אול, "to be strong." The primary mean-

---

23. Kaiser, *Isaiah 1–12*, 124.
24. Jensen, *Isaiah 1–39*, 113.
25. De Jong, *Isaiah among the Ancient Near Eastern Prophets*, 389.
26. Pope, *El in the Ugaritic Texts*, 1.
27. Ibid., 19.

ings of this root as used in biblical texts are "god" (pagan or false gods), "God" (the true God of Israel), and less frequently, "the mighty" (referring to people or angels).

Typically, אל is an appellative, with roughly the same semantic range as the term אלהים.[28] The word can therefore be preceded by the article: האל, "the [true] God" (e.g., Ps 18:31, 33, 48; 57:3). Like אל, אלהים can be employed in reference to an "alien god" (Deut 32:12; Mal 2:11) or a "strange god" (Ps 44:21; 81:10). Moreover, אל, not אלהים, is used when YHWH is contrasted with his people (Num 23:19; Isa 31:3; Ezek 28:9; Hos 11:9; Job 25:4).

Davidson has observed the pronounced tendency in Scripture to accompany אל with epithets. Indeed, as used in biblical texts, it must be concluded that the word is usually qualified by words or descriptions that further define the word. This leads Davidson to conclude that these qualifications both elevate the concept of אל in Scripture and distinguish the term as used biblically from others who might be so named.[29]

The Christian reading of messianic texts in the Hebrew Bible means that the translation of the term has become blemished with a reluctance to see either the Messiah or a future king as a warrior. The New Testament view of YHWH would also shy away from seeing the Hebrew גבור as meaning "Warrior" rather than more politically correct "mighty," so the sense of physical strength inherent in the term may be lost. Jenson is typical of some scholars who try to compensate the idea of a character with skills to take part in combat by referring back to the subsequent verse where we are assured that "his reign shall be one of endless peace."[30]

Eternal Father (אביעד)

Blenkinsopp notes that the "eternal Father is a rare but not unattested formation."[31] Two modes of thought categorize the reading of the term. First, the idea of "father" is one that looks to the past. This takes the well known idea of the patriarchal "father," whereby a person with this title would be seen not only as the head of the group, in the idea of ruler and governor, but also as protector of their heritage and faith, in the lines

---

28. Hartman, "God, Names of," 674.
29. Davidson, *Theology of the Old Testament*, 61.
30. Jensen, *Isaiah 1–39*, 113.
31. Blenkinsopp, *Isaiah 1–39*, 250.

of Abraham and Moses. The second mainstream idea is that "father" is a term that looks to the future. Obviously, if the designations refer to a newborn child, or a child whose birth is expected in the future, they are not a father in the biological or patriarchal sense, but rather seek to convey what his future role will be as leader of his people, with a legitimate and well recognized claim to this position as their "father." Clements suggests that the designation shows "the concern of the king for the welfare of his people."[32] The addition of the term "eternal" or "everlasting" would seem to be the typical acknowledgment that the king, whether in the divine or human realm, would have an everlasting or eternal life, for example in Ps 72:5, 17.

Prince of Peace (שר־שלום)

The designation "Prince of Peace" is a classic messianic designation that is used by both the Jewish and Christian communities. The focus of the majority of commentaries on the text is on the idea of the ushering in of a peaceful era by this new reign. Peace here does not merely mean that war will no longer be waged, though naturally this would be a necessity in terms of a stable and successful rule, but rather, as Brueggemann proposes, the notion is more likely tied up with imposing an "order on reality."[33] It is not the task of the people of Israel to restore or impose peace; rather it is the role of a governing leader. Jenson sees the designation as "the result and climax of the first three" as שלום would imply "the concept of fullness and completeness."[34] Kaiser notes that the term is "reminiscent of the divine name from Judg 6:24, 'Yahweh is peace'"[35] but fails as several commentators do to comment on the significance of the term שַׂר "prince." According to BDB this could be translated as chieftain, chief, ruler, official, captain or prince, so the immediate association with throne names may not be based on this final designation. The meaning is clear, however, as whatever role the referent takes, his position will be one of solid, dependable rule over his people who he will treat with respect and care befitting a ruler who has been bestowed a great honor in his role.

---

32. Clements, *Isaiah 1–39*, 108.
33. Brueggemann, *Isaiah 1–39*, 83.
34. Jensen, *Isaiah 1–39*, 113.
35. Kaiser, *Isaiah 1–12*, 129.

Commentators on the Text

In terms of the text of the verse in general, very few commentators question that the preceding verse speaks about the birth of a child through whom the house of David is assured that the line of succession will continue. However, in opposition to this traditional interpretation, several commentators, Wildberger for example, view the birth not as one in the distant and predictable future, but as having already occurred.[36] The simplest explanation for the use of this birth story is that following a period of hardship, a sudden change such as the birth of a royal heir would signal a change for the better. There appears to be no concrete evidence, certainly in the Hebrew Bible at least, that the birth of a crown prince would have been viewed as a salvific event. The key attitude of the Israelite faith—which as the norm kept its distance from the institution of kingship—would seem to reinforce the notion that the birth of a prince, even one who could claim to be heir to a throne, would not have attested any particular religious value. Nevertheless, those who would have been close to the royal family would have enthusiastically greeted a royal birth, as witnessed in ancient Egyptian culture and the Royal Psalms.[37]

Sweeney argues for the text as describing the accession rite of a king. He terms the poem as the "Royal Psalm of Thanksgiving" that presupposes the enthronement of a new Davidic king, in this case, Hezekiah.[38] Sweeney maintains that the reference to the child in the first part of the verse presupposes not the actual birth of a child, but Jerusalem's royal ideology that saw the Davidic monarch as the "son" of YHWH as in 2 Sam 7:14 and Ps 2:7. Secondly, the reference to the government being set on his shoulder indicates the inauguration of his authority.

Childs sides with Alt in terms of seeing the text as an accession oracle due to the presence of the throne titles. Nevertheless, he makes a strong case for distinguishing between the conventional language of the oracle and its biblical function within the book of Isaiah. He sees that any suggestion that the text is "simply hyperbolic, oriental language used to celebrate the accession of a new Israelite king is to historicize the biblical text and to overlook its role within the larger literary context."[39] Childs

---

36. Wildberger, *Isaiah 1–12*, 399.
37. Blenkinsopp, *History of Prophecy in Israel*, 109.
38. Sweeney, *Isaiah 1–39*, 182.
39. Childs, *Isaiah*, 80.

sees as crucial the need for any interpretation not to focus simply on the preliterary form of the text, since to interpret this text as "a historical vestige, moored in misguided hopes from Israel's past"[40] is to misinterpret the canonical forces that have formed the prophetic tradition into a body of Scripture directed to Israel's consequent generations of faith. In short, for Childs, the text may well reproduce the conventional language of its historical situation, but far more important for determining the meaning is to acknowledge the primarily eschatological development of the verses.

It is also significant that the death of Ahaz is only noted later on in the book of Isaiah, in 14:28. It seems more probable that a birth is being discussed, but we do not know the identity of the baby. Blenkinsopp makes a detailed analysis of this point, highlighting how, although the imagery in the poem is very vivid, it remains "unspecific enough to have permitted the poem to be recycled on successive occasion."[41] This weaken the arguments that many critics have put forward proposing a particular monarch or ruler.

Brueggemann concurs with critics who see the text as referring to the birth of an heir to the throne of David who is expected by the general population to be more effective than his predecessor. Brueggemann goes a step further than those who would see the birth as quite simply a cause for joy by stating that it would also be an apt occasion for royal propaganda and sees the series of titles as ritualized hyperbole.[42] The titles assert that the new king will meet every expectation of the populace and will perform every responsibility of the royal office. Thus the king will be shrewd, wise, and discerning in contrast to the foolishness of his predecessor.

Blenkinsopp highlights that there is a problem of form in this instance as in such rituals "the deity addresses the ruler-designate directly"[43] (see 2 Sam 7:14 and Ps 2:7), and does so in terms of the divine adoption of a son, neither of which is the case in the text here. More obviously, in terms of the form, only four names are conferred on the son in the poem, although some commentators have attempted to compose a fifth; for ex-

---

40. Ibid.
41. Blenkinsopp, *Isaiah 1–39*, 248.
42. Brueggemann, *Isaiah 1–39*, 83.
43. Blenkinsopp, *Isaiah 1–39*, 248.

ample, Wildberger suggests the name "great in sovereign authority"[44] has been omitted due to apparent damage to the text at the beginning of v. 6 though this does seem somewhat of a stretch. The Egyptian enthronement liturgies likewise grant the new king throne names that refer to the qualities desired of the new monarch similar to the designations that appear here. The fact that there are only four titles instead of the five does not negate the possibility of an analogy with Egyptian throne names, especially as the designations used are so out of synch with the apparently careful use of designations in the rest of the text of the book of Isaiah. Although the text refers to YHWH's victory over the oppressors as a past event in 9:1–4, the perspective of this psalm is future orientated, as indicated by the statement in 9:6 that, "The zeal of יהוה צבאות (YHWH of Hosts) will do this." YHWH's defeat of the new king's enemies in conjunction with the establishment of his kingship is a common motif in Jerusalem's royal ideology as can be seen in Egyptian politics. The concluding statement is YHWH guaranteeing support to the new ruler just as the Egyptian pharaoh would have had divine protection.

CONCLUSION

The initial reaction to the four designations that are present in v. 5 if one is to study the use of designations throughout the entire book of Isaiah is that they do not follow the normal, some might argue even deliberate, distribution of the designations throughout the text. The only title to appear elsewhere in the text of Isaiah is "mighty God" in 10:21. In this verse it appears as a lone title for YHWH and is not grouped with any other designations. All three traditional sections of the book of Isaiah groups names according to some particular structure, normally for the poetic effect of parallelism, or to enhance a particular aspect of the divine character.

The idea of the kingship of YHWH is stressed so heavily throughout the text that there would be no reason to demote his status to that of a prince or an heir. Therefore the four titles together must not be referring to YHWH. This leaves two other likely options, an earthy king or a messianic figure that is to appear in the future. De Jong best summarizes the argument that the designations do not refer to an earthly king: "read as eight-century prophecy, the portrayals of the ideal [earthly] king would

---

44. Wildberger, *Isaiah 1–12*, 412.

imply a rejection of the current king, and this was not part of Isaiah's message."[45] If we are to read the text as prophetic then the birth of this royal heir is, just as with Immanuel in 7:14, to be interpreted in the prophetic sense of a sign. It is not only an indicator that YHWH will act consistently, according to his promises, but is itself a reality.

In terms of the rather obvious question of "Are there not only four names in the text?," Clements has suggested that the fifth name had been "lost," though he does not elaborate on whether this was a deliberate omission or some sort of scribal error.[46] However, it may be taken that the "nomen" or birth name is not included, as the text is explicit in its grammatical reference to what name *will* be given to the child when he is made king. The influence therefore of the Egyptian throne names and accession rite of the king is clear on this text. The complex imagery and language associated with these titles was linked with ideas that the new king received the divine spirit and became a new "person" with a new "heart."[47] It was therefore fitting that the king should be given new throne names that were associated with command, equivalent with his influence in overseeing and governing YHWH's kingdom, just as the Egyptian kings had with the two lands of Egypt. The whole section is focused on an era where the people are experiencing considerable anguish as a result of foreign domination, under which a proportion of the people of Israel lost land to the conquering Assyrians.

Therefore, the royal rather than divine designations point towards a birth that will be no ordinary birth, and therefore will require a different announcement. The circumstance for celebration here is the birth of an heir to the throne. From the Isaiah's viewpoint, the birth that is depicted and announced in v. 5 is an indication of hope and positive anticipation. The ancient assurance that a son of King David will ascend the throne is reiterated. The designations allow an image of continuous harmony, governed with uprightness and fairness. We cannot find a definite referent of the designations in the text. Whoever this is will experience a birth that will be a signal of optimism and demonstrate assurance in the future of YHWH's relationship with his people.

---

45. De Jong, *Isaiah among the Ancient near Eastern Prophets*, 382.
46. Clements, *Isaiah 1–39*, 108.
47. Ibid., 107.

BIBLIOGRAPHY

Allen, James P. *Middle Egyptian: An Introduction to the Language and Culture of Hieroglyphs.* New York: Cambridge University Press, 2000.

Alt, Albrecht. "Jesaja 8:23—9:6: Befreiungsmacht und Kronungstag." In *Festschrift Alfred Bertholet zum 80. Geburtstag,* edited by Walter Baumgartner, 206-25. Tübingen: Mohr/Siebeck, 1950. Reprinted in Albrecht Alt, *Kleine Schriften zur Geschichte des Volkes Israel,* edited by Martin Noth, 2:206-25. Munich: Beck, 1953.

Blenkinsopp, Joseph. *A History of Prophecy in Israel.* 2nd ed. Louisville: Westminster John Knox, 1996.

———. *Isaiah 1-39.* Anchor Bible 19. New York: Doubleday, 2000.

Brueggemann, Walter. *Isaiah 1-39.* Westminster Bible Companion. Louisville: Westminster John Knox, 1998.

Byrne, Máire. "'My People Shall Know My Name': The Divine Designations in the Book of Isaiah as a Hermeneutical Key to the Formation of the Text in Its Final Form." PhD diss., St. Patrick's College, Maynooth, 2007.

Childs, Brevard S. *Isaiah.* Old Testament Library. Louisville: Westminster John Knox, 2001.

Clements, R. E. *Isaiah 1-39.* New Century Bible Commentary. Grand Rapids: Eerdmans, 1980.

David, A. Rosalie. *Handbook to Life in Ancient Egypt.* Oxford: Oxford University Press, 1999.

Davidson, Andrew. *The Theology of the Old Testament.* Edinburgh: T. & T. Clark, 1907.

Delitzsch, Franz. *Biblical Commentary on the Prophecies of Isaiah.* Edinburgh: T. & T. Clark, 1890.

Gardiner, Alan Henderson. *Egyptian Grammar: Being an Introduction to the Study of Hieroglyphs.* 3rd ed. Oxford: Griffith Institute, Ashmolean Museum, 1957.

Hartman, Louis. "God, Names of." In *Encyclopedia Judaica,* 7:674-83. Jerusalem: Macmillan, 1972.

Hastings, James et al., editors. *Encyclopaedia of Religion and Ethics.* Vol. 1. Edinburgh: T. & T. Clark, 1917.

Jensen, Joseph. *Isaiah 1-39.* Old Testament Message 8. Wilmington, DE: Glazier, 1984.

Jensen, Robin Margaret. *Understanding Early Christian Art.* London: Routledge, 2000.

Jong, Matthijs J de. *Isaiah among the Ancient Near Eastern Prophets: A Comparative Study of the Earliest Stages of the Isaiah Tradition and the Neo-Assyrian Prophecies.* Vetus Testamentum Supplements 117. Leiden: Brill, 2007.

Kaiser, Otto. *Isaiah 1-12: A Commentary.* Translated by R. A. Wilson. Old Testament Library. Philadelphia: Westminster, 1972.

O'Connor, David, and David P. Silverman. *Ancient Egyptian Kingship.* Probleme der Ägyptologie 9. Leiden: Brill, 1995.

Pentiuc, Eugen J. *Jesus the Messiah in the Hebrew Bible.* New York: Paulist, 2006.

Pinch, Geraldine. *Egyptian Mythology: A Guide to the Gods, Goddesses, and Traditions of Ancient Egypt.* Oxford: Oxford University Press, 2004.

Pope, Marvin. *El in the Ugaritic Texts.* Vetus Testamentum Supplements 2. Leiden: Brill, 1955.

Rad, Gerhard von. "Das judäische Königsritual." *Theologische Literaturzeitung* 72/4 (1947) 211-16. Reprinted in Gerhard von Rad, *Gesammelte Studien zum Alten Testament,* 205-13, Munich: Kaiser, 1958.

———. "The Royal Ritual in Judah." In *From Genesis to Chronicles: Explorations in Old Testament Theology*, 167–73. Translated by E. W. Trueman Dicken. Edited by K. C. Hanson. Fortress Classics in Biblical Studies. Minneapolis: Fortress, 2005.

Roberts, J. J. M. "Whose Child Is This? Reflections on the Speaking Voice in Isaiah 9:5." *Harvard Theological Review* 90 (1997) 115–30. Reprinted in J. J. M. Roberts, *The Bible and the Ancient Near East: Collected Essays*, 143–56. Winona Lake, IN: Eisenbrauns, 2002.

Sawyer, John F. A. *The Fifth Gospel: Isaiah in the History of Christianity*. Cambridge: Cambridge University Press, 1996.

Shafer, Byron E., et al., editors. *Religion in Ancient Egypt: Gods, Myths, and Personal Practice*. Ithaca, NY: Cornell University Press, 1991.

Shaw, Ian. *The Oxford History of Ancient Egypt*. Oxford: Oxford University Press, 2000.

Sweeney, Marvin A. *Isaiah 1–39: With an Introduction to Prophetic Literature*. Forms of the Old Testament Literature 16. Grand Rapids: Eerdmans, 1996.

Wildberger, Hans. *Isaiah 1–12: A Commentary*. Translated by Thomas H. Trapp. Continental Commentaries. Minneapolis: Fortress, 1991.

Wilkinson, Toby A. H. *Early Dynastic Egypt*. Paperback ed. London: Routledge, 2001.

Woolley, Reginald Maxwell. *Coronation Rites*. Cambridge Handbooks of Liturgical Study. Cambridge: Cambridge University Press, 1915.

7

Jesus and Yeshua

Jewish Interpretations of the Gospels and Its Impact on Jewish-Christian Dialogue

Peter Admirand

INTRODUCTION

UNDERSTANDABLY, JEWISH INTERPRETATIONS OF Christ have traditionally been non-existent or unflattering. After Christian charges, slanders, pogroms, and ultimately, genocide against the Jews proliferated, decades of relative peace and amity had to occur for any hope of genuine dialogue. As Michael S. Kogan writes in *Opening the Covenant: A Jewish Theology of Christianity*: "But how can Jews be expected to see the hand of God in the spread of a faith whose adherents so often denigrated Judaism and frequently persecuted Jews? Will Jews be able to separate the positive aspects of Christianity from the negative, and from the sinful acts of Christians toward Jews?"[1]

In the roughly sixty-five years since the closing of the last Nazi concentration camps, we have seen incremental, if still-promising, steps forward on the Christian side with the publication of *Nostra Aetate*, the "1975 Vatican Guidelines for Catholic-Jewish Relations," and similar documents by the World Council of Churches.[2] Christian theologians

---

1. Kogan, *Opening the Covenant*, xiv.

2. It must be said, of course, that recent years (as of July 17, 2010) have not been auspicious ones in Catholic-Jewish dialogue, with a number of blunders on the Catholic side,

such as John Pawlikowski, Paul Van Buren, A. Roy Eckhart, Rosemary Radford Reuther, and Didier Pollefeyt have challenged or examined the meaning and identity of the Christ-event and the uniqueness of Christ and how that bears upon Jewish-Christian relations, particularly after the Shoah.³ Key areas of examination have included the Jewishness of Jesus; the question of a single, double, or alternative covenant model; the moral errors of supersessionist theology (also known as the theology of substitution); the important and clear distinctions between "Christologies of Discontinuity" as opposed to "Christologies of Continuity"; the "end of christological salvation triumphalism";⁴ the moral, historical and theological errors (and repercussion) of the deicide charge against the Jewish people; the expectations and fulfilment of the Messiah; and the "newness" and the uniqueness of Christ in light of the on-going Jewish covenant. On the Jewish side, the publication of *Dabru Emet* ("Speak the Truth") should be considered a watershed event, though a number of engaging Jewish scholars (including Franz Rosenzweig, Martin Buber, and Irving Greenberg) laid a solid foundation that helped to make such a document possible.

In this paper I will ultimately focus on two works, Jacob Neusner's *A Rabbi Talks with Jesus* and the sections that examine that work in Pope Benedict XVI's *Jesus of Nazareth*, and how this interaction positively and negatively bears on Jewish-Christian dialogue. I also, however, want to include Peter Schäfer's *Jesus in the Talmud*, both because it is an important work to highlight in the study of Jewish-Christian relations and because it can serve as a helpful foil and backdrop to the discussion here. My attempt, therefore, is by no means meant to be exhaustive but to concentrate upon two recent works of Jewish scholarship and writing on Jesus

---

from the initial attempt to reinstate a bishop who denied the Shoah to the U.S. Catholic Bishops initially removing a line from an Adult Catechism because it spoke of the eternal Jewish covenant.

3. For relevant works on post-Holocaust Christologies see Pawlikowski, "Search for a New Paradigm for the Christian-Jewish Relationship"; Pawlikowski, *Jesus and the Theology of Israel*; Pawlikowski, *Christ in the Light of the Christian-Jewish Dialogue*; Pollefeyt, "Church and the Jews"; Pollefeyt, "Christology after Auschwitz"; Pollefeyt, *Jews and Christians*; Bruteau, *Jesus Through Jewish Eyes*; Foley, "Heir or Orphan"; Haas, "Judaism in Protestant Encounters with the Shoah"; Kogan, *Opening the Covenant*; Cunningham, et al., *Catholic Church and the Jewish People*.

4. Pollefeyt, "Christology after Auschwitz," 233.

and the response to one of these works by Benedict XVI in the context of Jewish-Christian dialogue.[5]

JESUS IN THE TALMUD

In Peter Schäfer's volume, *Jesus in the Talmud*, Schäfer examines the scant but still fascinating Talmudic material that mentions—or seems to allude to—Jesus of Nazareth. In the work, Schäfer argues that the few passages dealing with Jesus are all

> polemical counternarratives that parody the New Testament stories, most notably the story of Jesus' birth and death. They ridicule Jesus' birth from a virgin, as maintained by the Gospels of Matthew and Luke, and they contest fervently the claim that Jesus is the Messiah and the Son of God. Most remarkably, they counter the New Testament Passion story with its message of the Jews' guilt and shame as Christ killers. Instead, they reverse it completely: yes, they maintain, we accept responsibility for it, but there is no reason to feel ashamed because we rightfully executed a blasphemer and idolater.[6]

Jesus, for example, is often referred to in these Talmudic passages as Yeshua ben Pandera/Pantera, claiming that Jesus was a bastard son of a tryst between his mother Miriam (Mary) and a Roman soldier, Pandera/Pantera. A similar argument can be found in Origen's *Contra Celsus*. Such claims of course strike down any notions that Jesus is the Son of God and undercut any salvific (or virginal) role of Mary. Other passages, according to Schäfer, link Jesus with the "disciple who turned out badly," implying that Jesus, like his mother, engaged in sexual misconduct,[7] but also dabbled in magic (especially based on his days in Egypt), and committed blasphemous and idolatrous acts. Furthermore, the passion narrative in the Gospels, as noted above, is altered, as Jesus is stoned to death and then hanged for his blasphemous and idolatrous behavior. Perhaps misinterpreting Pilate's hesitation to execute Jesus in the Gospels, a passage in the Bavli claims that the matter and process of Jesus's execution was distinctive as his sentence was announced forty days before it was

---

5. For a helpful historical overview on Jewish perceptions of Jesus, see Cook, "Evolving Jewish Views of Jesus."

6. Schäfer, *Jesus in the Talmud*, 9.

7. Ibid., 28.

carried out, to give ample time for defenders to come to his cause, and because he clearly was close to the government.[8] Such a claim also negates Jesus's prophesying his death to the disciples if it were publicly known. Nevertheless, for some rabbis, Jesus deserved death. The crime was fitting. Schäfer writes: "With this deliberate 'misreading' of the New Testament narrative, the Bavli (re)claims Jesus for the Jewish people—but only to fend off once and for all any claim by himself or his followers. Yes, indeed, the Bavli admits, Jesus was a Jewish heretic, who was quite successful in seducing many of us. But he was taken care of according to the Jewish law, got what he deserved—and that's the end of the story."[9]

Speaking of ends—at least ignominious ones—Jesus is said to be eternally languishing in hell, boiled in excrement. "For the master has said: Whoever mocks the words of the Sages is punished with boiling excrement."[10] It need not be said that such a depiction stands in contrast to the Gospel version(s).

MORE FAVORABLE INTERPRETATIONS

Just as most Christians no longer adhere to the erroneous charge of deicide against the Jews or claim God's covenant with the Jewish people has been revoked or replaced, Christ eternally boiling in excrement is not, of course, held by any Jews sincerely engaged in Jewish-Christian dialogue. In this section, I want to note a few Jewish theologians who have played crucial roles in laying the foundation for Jewish-Christian dialogue on the Jewish side. Before touching on some contemporary figures, I need to note, as Ignaz Maybaum reminds us, how "Judah Hallevi and Maimonides s[aw] Judaism as the seed which br[ought] forth the tree with two branches, Christianity and Islam."[11] As Maybaum clarifies, however, "The metaphor of the seed and tree can, indeed must, be understood by the post-medieval Jew as meaning that Christianity and Islam are within Judaism." [12]Note that Maybaum has Franz Rosenzweig's *Star of Redemption* in mind in particular, again showing how each generation grapples with their predecessors. As Kogan writes: "Rosenzweig's most familiar images are of

---

8. Ibid., 65.
9. Ibid., 72.
10. Quoted in ibid., 85.
11. Maybaum, "Secular and Holy," in *Ignaz Maybaum: A Reader*, 127.
12. Ibid., 127.

the Star of Redemption, with Judaism as the eternal flame in the heart of the star and Christianity as the eternal rays shining out in the world."[13] Such imagery of connection and interrelatedness help to heal many of the genuine wounds between both groups. Likewise, Martin Buber's phrasing of "Jesus, my great brother" had great impact in encouraging and challenging Jews to take a second look at the Jewishness of Jesus. A relatively recent work like *Jesus through Jewish Eyes*, a collection of rabbis writing about Jesus, attests to the positive advances in Jewish-Christian dialogue. While at times highly (and not always accurately) critical of Christianity, Alan Berger and David Patterson's *Jewish-Christian Dialogue: Drawing Honey from the Rock* also deserves attention, particularly its section titled "The Jewish Jesus"[14] and the chapter that includes a transcripted dialogue with Christian scholars David Gushee, John Pawlikowski, and John Roth. Michael Kogan's work (mentioned above) may, in many ways, be the most important contribution by a Jewish individual to the debate. Kogan, a believing Jew, wants to argue that there is no reason for Jews to reject the notion that Jesus was sent by God to bring the Word to the Gentiles (though he is clear that the Jewish covenant remains valid).[15]

Arguably, the trend running through many contemporary Jewish participants in the Jewish-Christian dialogue seems best represented in the following statement of Ignaz Maybaum: "The study of the difference between Judaism and Christianity is the heart and soul of any Jewish-Christian dialogue worthy of the name."[16] Berger and Patterson, for example, write: "The perspective presented [within *Jewish-Christian Dialogue*] is admittedly Jewish. It is likely that Christians will have a different perspective. In any case, our hope is that this Jewish perspective will add depth to the Jewish-Christian dialogue. Indeed, the differences in perspectives are essential to this dialogue that seeks a next step."[17]

While Kogan emphasizes how Jesus brings Gentiles to the biblical God, thus underscoring great similarities in the Jewish and Christian moral and spiritual messages, he is also clear that the covenants remain

---

13. Kogan, *Opening the Covenant*, 88.
14. Berger and Patterson, *Jewish Christian Dialogue*, 74–81.
15. Kogan, *Opening the Covenant*, 232.
16. Maybaym, "Trialogue between Jew, Christian, and Muslim," 96.
17. Berger and Patterson, *Jewish Christian Dialogue*, 73.

distinct. Touching upon such differences, Irving Greenberg has provocatively written:

> As extraordinary as their tradition is and as blessed with Divine Presence as they feel they are, Christians can acknowledge modestly that their gifts do not exhaust the infinite presence and blessing of the Lord. Christians need not cease sharing their exaltation with others; they need only give up the implied arrogance that no other faith communities can equally experience God in their midst ... One wing of this approach may choose to focus more on Jesus bringing people to God rather than on Jesus as the self-contained, exclusive manifestation of the Divine.[18]

In light of recognizing such differences (without of course undermining the common interests that *Dabru Emet* highlights),[19] I will now turn to Jacob Neusner's *A Rabbi Talks with Jesus*. Believing the most profound compliment he can give someone is to listen, engage, and debate one's ideas,[20] Neusner imagines himself listening to the Sermon on the Mount as a first century Jew to trace why and whether he would follow Jesus, or return home to his wife, children, and dog and continue his study and living of the Torah.

"COME LET US REASON TOGETHER"[21]

Rabbi Neusner wrote *A Rabbi Talks with Jesus* (1993, rev. 2000, reprinted 2001, 2007) because of his profound respect and care for the many Christians he has known and been friends with. His aims are for Christians to become more faithful and enlightened Christians and for Jews to have a greater understanding of their unique identity and religion. Though aware of much scholarly and biblical exegesis, he focuses his thoughts primarily on his reading of Matthew's Gospel. As he writes: "An argument with Matthew's Jesus is only plausible because there really is a shared Torah between us, so we can agree sufficiently on the main thing to disagree on other things."[22] In the course of this work, therefore, Neusner explains "in

---

18. Greenberg, "Covenantal Partners in a Postmodern World," 67.

19. Berger and Patterson write: "Dabru Emet's optimistic assessment—while laudable in its intent—is purchased at a steep price: the peril of theological evasion and historical distortion" (*Jewish-Christian Dialogue*, 170).

20. Neusner, *Rabbi Talks with Jesus*, 20.

21. This is the title of chapter 1 in ibid.

22. Ibid., 8.

a very straightforward and unapologetic way why, if [he] had been in the Land of Israel in the first century, [he] would not have joined the circle of Jesus' disciples."[23] While respectful of much of what Jesus says, Neusner will not follow select Jews in previous eras who praise Jesus as a Rabbi or "Galilean miracle worker" because "these evasions of the Christian claim to truth will serve no more ... I will not praise with excessive, irrelevant compliments someone else's God: it is demeaning and dishonest."[24] What results is a fascinating (and sometimes frustrating) interpretation for a Christian reader.

Neusner predominantly focuses his examination of various passages in Matthew, such as 5:17–20, which begins: "Think not that I have come to abolish the Torah and the prophets; I have come not to abolish them, but to fulfil them. For truly, I say to you, till heaven and earth pass away, not an iota, not a dot will pass from the Torah until all is accomplished." While Neusner is clear that the great teachers of Torah "teach, explain, extend, amplify, and enrich" and do not simply "repeat or paraphrase,"[25] he contends that Jesus, ultimately, and repeatedly demands a clear choice: Jesus or Torah? In the Beatitudes, for example, Jesus speaks of how blessed are those persecuted for his sake; elsewhere he also calls on Jews to break the fourth and fifth commandments, if necessary, to follow him. While Jews could make study of the Torah take precedence over an obligation to parents, Jesus is clear that the obligation is in following him, which seems to set him above the Torah, the law that God has passed on to God's people. Neusner also takes umbrage at the story of the rich man who asks Jesus what he needs to gain eternal life. After they agree on what could be the core moral teachings of the Hebrew Scriptures, Jesus says to be perfect one must sell all he or she has for the poor, and come and follow him. Neusner cannot see how following the core precepts of the Torah would not be perfection itself, nor how such practices would not disrupt all of society if there is no stable family life (which God and Torah bless as sanctified). He also is amazed that Jesus repeatedly addresses the individual, but not the community, leaving out a crucial connection with his quote from Leviticus that specifically addresses the people of Israel. Neusner comments: "That is why, in my mind, what Jesus has not said

23. Ibid., 3.
24. Ibid., 32.
25. Ibid., 43.

takes on profound weight; he has spoken to me, but not to us; there is no dimension of the holy and eternal Israel in his reading of the Torah's fundamental teaching."[26] Articulating the difference between the path of following Jesus or Torah, Neusner elsewhere clarifies: "Any (in that time, male; but today, male or female) Israelite can master the Torah and become a sage, but only Jesus can be Jesus Christ."[27]

Regarding the various mitzvots pertaining to the Sabbath (which Jesus's disciples violate by picking the grains of wheat), Neusner emphasizes that such rules are "not silly prohibitions; they form the this-worldly expressions of that act of sanctification that imitates God's sanctification of the Seventh Day."[28] For Neusner, the issue is Jesus's authority to call for such radical changes and reinterpretations. Imagining he is talking to Jesus's disciples, Neusner writes: "So I say to the disciple, is it really so that your master, the son of man, is lord of the Sabbath? Then—so I asked before, so I ask again—is your master God? And that forms the crux of the matter."[29]

A POPE AND RABBI IN DIALOGUE

In *Jesus of Nazareth*, Pope Benedict XVI's calls Neusner a "great Jewish scholar,"[30] and so turns to *A Rabbi Talks with Jesus* "to be guided toward a better understanding of the authentic Jewishness and the mystery of Jesus."[31] Although the compliments are noteworthy, already one should be on guard. While Neusner acknowledges "Jesus knows the Torah at least as well as anybody else,"[32] the Jewishness of Jesus is placed in radical difference and opposition to the Torah. Salvation trumps sanctification; moral right annuls ritual rites; the heavenly kingdom of the future overshadows present, daily, human life. According to Neusner: "Jesus Christ in Matthew's gospel speaks of everything but the social order of the here and now."[33] And as Neusner adds toward the end of his book: "Jesus and

26. Ibid., 96.
27. Ibid., 66.
28. Ibid., 82.
29. Ibid., 88.
30. Benedict, *Jesus of Nazareth*, 69.
31. Ibid., 70.
32. Neusner, *Rabbi Talks with Jesus*, 96–97.
33. Ibid., 103.

his disciples went their way, off the stage of Israel's enduring life."[34] How, therefore, do we interpret the Jewishness of Jesus in light of Neusner's arguments? It must be clarified that one of Benedict's principal aims in his work is to argue that claims of Christ's divine and unique status originate from Jesus within the Gospels and Christian tradition. Benedict therefore argues against those thinkers who have tried to contend that Christological titles were developed or created in a post-Jesus context.[35] Neusner's reading of Matthew supports the Pope's contention, as Neusner cannot follow Christ precisely because he reads Matthew's Jesus as setting himself above the Torah; in essence, claiming to be (or have the authority of) God.[36]

Benedict does, however, equally make (if also subjective) responses to Neusner. Benedict acknowledges that if Jesus is not God, then indeed, Neusner is right to question how Jesus can call on Israel to violate two commandments to follow him. However, building upon the notion that God has chosen Israel to be a light unto the nations, Benedict (echoing a number of theologians like Paul Van Buren in this debated matter), stresses how Christ brought the Word of God to the Gentiles—giving the "gift of universality"[37]—thus reformulating what it means to be a "new family."[38] Benedict also claims that Neusner is right to notice that Jesus challenges the role of the Sabbath, but he claims:

> Now, Jesus' intention is not to abolish either the family or the Sabbath-as-celebration-of-creation, but he has to create a broader context for both. It is true that his invitation to join him as a member of a new and universal family through sharing his obedience to the Father does at first break up the social order of Israel. But from her very inception, the Church that emerged, and continues to emerge, has attached fundamental importance to defending the family as the core of all social order . . . The fight for Sunday is another of the Church's major concerns in the present day, when there is so much to upset the rhythm of time that sustains community.[39]

34. Ibid., 157.
35. Benedict, *Jesus of Nazareth*, 354–55.
36. Ibid., 106–7.
37. Ibid., 116.
38. Ibid., 117.
39. Ibid., 120–21.

While Benedict again emphasizes that Jesus (as God Incarnate) opens the covenant to the entire world, he does not address the unfortunate move by the Catholic Church to share no longer the same period of Sabbath observance as Jews. Nor does he assess and clarify the role of the ongoing relationship and covenant of the Jewish people. While his "dialogue" with Neusner is promising, ultimately, it is a missed opportunity for reconciliation and mutual clarification.

CONCLUSION: EMBRACING SIMILARITY, ARTICULATING DIFFERENCE

Irving Greenberg has called Jesus a failed (as opposed to false) Messiah, intending such a term to be complimentary and ironic,[40] especially as he links a sense of failure to Moses and Abraham. Calling Jesus a failed messiah is to acknowledge that the world still needs to be saved. Christians, of course, can still embrace such a term while speaking of the Holy Spirit to guide and enflame believers to continue the work of Christ in establishing the Reign of God in our midst, to use the language of many liberation theologians. Or as Didier Pollefeyt writes: "Christians must agree with Jews that the world is not yet redeemed."[41] Clearly, Christians are called to humble themselves (and some of their doctrinal and theological claims), to acknowledge (and take comfort in) the fact that "their gifts do not exhaust the infinite presence and blessing of the Lord" as Greenberg noted above.[42] Speaking as a Catholic theologian, would I want to imagine a world in which goodness and holiness were only possible if it came through believing Christians? Surely not.

Jews and Christians, coming together in dialogue and community, must, of course, try to appreciate areas of confluence, but must all the more articulate and clarify their doctrinal differences, that most importantly, must never take precedence when one is encountering the face of the other, an other who calls out to us and obligates us (in Levanasian terms) to respond. Too often, Christians have failed in this response and

---

40. Greenberg, "Toward an Organic Model of The Relationship," 153.
41. Pollefeyt, "Church and the Jews," 142.
42. See also my essays: Admirand, "Healing the Distorted Face"; Admirand, "Theological Memory in the Face of Tragedy and Mass Atrocity"; and Admirand, "Amidst Fractured Faith and the Fragility of Reason."

so must enter any interfaith dialogue without the false trappings of doctrinal superiority.[43]

Before concluding, I need to state that another article could be spent clarifying (or debating) some of Neusner's interpretations of certain Gospel passages. In one such area, Benedict XVI, reflecting his unfortunate and unnecessary agonic battle with liberation theology, agrees with Neusner who "discerningly critiques from a Jewish perspective . . . the absence of the whole social dimension in Jesus' preaching."[44] Benedict is right in noting the "epoch-making event" in which "the political and social order is released from the directly sacred realm, from theocratic legislation, and is transferred to the freedom of man."[45] He also, therefore, is correct to imply the need for every society to uphold religious freedom for all and to avoid a theocracy of any kind. Nevertheless, turning to passages of Torah as a guide for such human, secular legislation or to the option for the poor and the call to grapple with structural and individual sin in liberation theology, would have helped to further clarify his point (and bring him closer to learning from the Jewish tradition as he set forth to do). Of course, one of the benefits of inter-faith dialogue is that it also stimulates intra-faith dialogue. Hopefully, some of the thinkers discussed here will do precisely just that.

---

43. See Admirand, "Interfaith Dialogue as Presence, Gift and Obligation."
44. Benedict, Jesus of Nazareth, 118.
45. Ibid.

BIBLIOGRAPHY

Admirand, Peter. "Theological Memory in the Face of Tragedy and Mass Atrocity." In *Facing Tragedies*, edited by Christopher Hamilton, Otto Neumaier, Gottfried Schweiger, and Clemens Sedmak, 129–38. Vienna: Lit-Verlag, 2009.

———. "Interfaith Dialogue as Presence, Gift and Obligation." *Teaching Religious Education* 4 (2009) 6–9. Online: http://www.slss.ie/resources/c/1233/TeachingRE%20Issue%204.pdf.

———. "Healing the Distorted Face: Doctrinal Reinterpretation(s) and the Christian Response to the Other." *One in Christ* 42 (2008) 302–17.

———. "Amidst Fractured Faith and the Fragility of Reason." *New Blackfriars*, forthcoming. Available at: http://www3.interscience.wiley.com/journal/123581455/abstract.

Benedict XVI. *Jesus of Nazareth: From the Baptism in the Jordan to the Transfiguration*. Translated by Adrian J. Walker. New York: Doubleday, 2007.

Berger, Alan L. and Patterson, David. *Jewish-Christian Dialogue: Drawing Honey from the Rock*. St. Paul: Paragon, 2008.

Bruteau, Beatrice, editor. *Jesus through Jewish Eyes: Rabbis and Scholars Engage an Ancient Brother in a New Conversation*. Maryknoll, NY: Orbis, 2003.

Cook, Michael. "Evolving Jewish Views of Jesus." In *Jesus through Jewish Eyes: Rabbis and Scholars Engage an Ancient Brother in a New Conversation*, edited by Beatrice Bruteau, 3–24. Maryknoll, NY: Orbis, 2003.

Cunningham, Phillip A., Norbert Hofmann, and Joseph Sievers. *The Catholic Church and the Jewish People: Recent Reflections from Rome*. Abrahamic Dialogue Series. New York: Fordham University Press, 2007.

Foley, Elena Procario. "Heir or Orphan: Theological Evolution and Devolution before and after *Nostra Aetate*." In *Vatican II Forty Years Later*, edited by William Madges, 308–39. Maryknoll, NY: Orbis, 2006.

Greenberg, Irving. *For the Sake of Heaven and Earth: The New Encounter between Judaism and Christianity*. Philadelphia: Jewish Publication Society, 2004.

Haas, Peter J. "Judaism in Protestant Encounters with the Shoah [with Critiques and Response]." In *Fire in the Ashes: God, Evil, and the Holocaust*, edited by David Patterson and John K. Roth, 59–83. Seattle: University of Washington Press, 2005.

Kogan, Michael S. *Opening the Covenant: A Jewish Theology of Christianity*. Oxford: Oxford University Press, 2008.

Maybaum, Ignaz. *Ignaz Maybaum: A Reader*. Edited by Nicholas de Lange. New York: Berghan, 2001.

Neusner, Jacob. *A Rabbi Talks with Jesus*. Rev. ed. Montreal: McGill-Queen's University Press, 2007.

Pawlikowski, John. "The Search for a New Paradigm for the Christian-Jewish Relationship: A Response to Michael Singer." In *Reinterpreting Revelation and Tradition: Jews and Christians in Conversation*. Edited by John T. Pawlikowski and Hayim Goren Perelmuter, 25–48. Franklin, WI: Sheed & Ward, 2000.

———. *Jesus and the Theology of Israel*. Zacchaeus Studies. Wilmington, DE: Glazer, 1989

———. *Christ in the Light of the Christian-Jewish Dialogue*. Studies in Judaism and Christianity. New York: Paulist, 1982.

Pollefeyt, Didier. "Christology after Auschwitz: A Catholic Perspective." In *Jesus Then & Now: Images of Jesus in History and Christology*, edited by Marvin Meyer and Charles Hughes, 229–48. Harrisburg, PA: Trinity, 2001.

———. "The Church and the Jews: Unsolvable Paradox or Unfinished Story?" In *Nostra Aetate: Origins, Promulgation, Impact on Jewish-Christian Relations*, edited by Neville Lamdan and Alberto Melloni, 131–44. Christianity and History. John XXIII Foundation for Religious Studies in Bologna 5. Berlin: Lit-Verlag, 2007.

Pollefeyt, Didier, editor. *Jews and Christians: Rivals or Partners for the Kingdom of God? In Search of An Alternative for the Theology of Substitution*. Louvain Theological and Pastoral Monographs 21. Louvain: Peeters, 1997.

Schäfer, Peter. *Jesus in the Talmud*. Princeton: Princeton University Press, 2007.

8

1 Peter as Biblical Proto-Theodicy

Reconciling Suffering Communities and Faithful Creator

RICHARD I. KUEH

INTRODUCTION

THIS PAPER SEEKS TO offer a somewhat nuanced approach to Petrine studies. In developing the idea of *paraenesis* (readily found in the critical study of 1 Peter), it further seeks to elucidate the purpose of 1 Peter by means of a category often cited in philosophical or systematic theologies: *theodicy*. The resultant claim would be that 1 Peter constitutes, in part, a practical theodicy to the recipients of the letter.

Of course, this is not possible without building upon some type of exegetical reconstruction of the situation of the letter's addressees. Suffice it to say, that is not a straightforward task, and it is further riddled with critical and hermeneutical difficulties. Therefore the first function of the paper is to demonstrate the reality of the readers' suffering, to reject theories that marginalize this claim, and to attempt to identify the nature of that suffering. The reality of this suffering will highlight the severity of the recipients' situation and, in turn, demonstrate the profundity of a paradox that the author attempts to resolve.

Recent studies of 1 Peter have demonstrated how the letter functions paraenetically in order to encourage the recipients of the letter. Broadly speaking, "paraenesis" is an umbrella term that recognises that some works of this epistolary literary genre function as *encouragement* to their recipients. This much is indicated by the letter itself: the author describes his own activity in writing to his correspondents in 1 Pet 5:12 with the participle παρακαλῶν ("encouraging"). In this context, paraenesis constitutes encouragement of suffering Christians, to persevere in their lifestyle and, most importantly, faith. Above all, the writer is concerned with Christians, who are suffering for being Christian, not to renounce Christianity, but to remain Christian in their circumstances.

Whereas much attention has been given to demonstrating the way in which the author is concerned with heartening the addressees with this paraenesis, little or no attention has been given to the notion that the author is concerned with "reconciling" the experiences of suffering communities with the faithfulness of their Creator.

"Reconciliation," of course, has a broad semantic range, but a specific meaning is intended here. By "reconciling" I do not suggest a verb with a redemptive force, a classic Pauline example of which is found in Rom 5:10: "For if while we were enemies, κατηλλάγημεν (we were reconciled, from the verb καταλλάσσω) to God through the death of his Son, much more surely, καταλλαγέντες (having been reconciled) will we be saved by his life." In fact, this idea of redemptive reconciliation (though itself not part of 1 Peter's vocabulary) is already presupposed in the letter: "You know that you were ransomed from the futile ways inherited from your ancestors, not with perishable things like silver or gold, but with the precious blood of Christ" (1 Pet 1:18–19a).

Rather, "reconciling" is meant with a similar force to the Latin verb in the title of Luis de Molina's famous sixteenth-century text: the "Concordia." Whereas Molina claims to have reconciled (*concordia*) free will (*liberi arbitrii*) with divine characteristics,[1] 1 Peter, I would argue, attempts to reconcile the recipients' circumstances with the goodness of God. In this sense, 1 Peter constitutes a deeply practical theodicy: theodicy in so far as it aims to address, and indeed resolve, the paradox of God's character and the suffering of the addressees; practical in so far as the inauspicious circumstances of the recipients are an empirical reality.

---

1. Molina's work engages with the divine characteristics of foreknowledge/knowledge (*divina praescientia*) as well as providence (*providentia*). For a good English translation, see Fredosso, trans., *On Divine Foreknowledge (Molina's Concordia)*.

THE CIRCUMSTANCES OF THE READERS

By means of prolegomenon, it should be stated that the recipients ought properly to be described in the plural as "communities." The greeting maintains that the Petrine communities are located in Pontus, Galatia, Cappadocia, Asia and Bithynia. This is a relatively vast area of land. Michaels states that the area comprised roughly 300,000 square miles.[2] According to Achtemeier, it covered at the very least the northern half of Asia Minor; north and west of the Tarsus Mountains.[3] The geographical place names are also attested Roman provinces, which according to early sources, were considered as a unit.[4] 1 Peter is, quite simply, addressed to a wide group of early Christian communities and, though it does suggest circumstances common to all these communities, it lacks reference to the situations of specific churches.

There have been, in my opinion, some rather eccentric attempts to use vocabulary and themes within the letter to narrow down the location of the target audience. Tàrrech considers that the Petrine community was located in a rural location, owing to a special employment of appropriate rural images that would be understood by a corresponding population. The metaphor of σπορᾶς (1 Pet 1:23) in addition to the fauna similes in the Isa 40:6–8 quotation of 1 Pet 1:24–25 apparently produce an "analogie fort connue et compréhensible."[5] Yet such a vast geographical location would have to include both rural areas (especially northern Galatia) as well as affluent urban areas in western Asia.

The letter is also addressed παρεπιδήμοις διασπορᾶς (1 Pet 1:1). The term διασπορᾶς might suggest that the recipients were Jews of the Dispersion. Much debate has ensued about the ethnic or racial composition of the correspondents. Though the letter is saturated with imagery and quotations from the Hebrew Bible (thus perhaps indicative of a Jewish audience), there are significant markers within the text that suggest otherwise. In their pre-Christian lives, the readers existed in a ματαίας

---

2. Michaels, *1 Peter*, 4.
3. Achtemeier, *1 Peter*, 50.
4. Strabo *Geography* 2.5.31; Dio Casius *History Rome* 71.23.
5. Tàrrech in Bechtler, *Following in His Steps*, 74. Against Tàrrech, the significance of the Isaianic passage is that it participates in 1 Peter's general affinity for Deutero-Isaianic quotations. Additionally, elaborate metaphorical language used elsewhere in the letter, e.g., "purify gold" (1 Pet 1:7) and "silver and gold" (1 Pet 1:18) counterbalances and offsets this notion.

ἀναστροφῆς (1 Pet 1:18). Suffice it to say, a "vain manner of life" or "futile ways" indicates a pagan or Gentile background. Moreover, the recipients were, according the author's employment of Hos 1:9, "once not a people" (1 Pet 2:10); hardly a fitting description of Judaism. Furthermore, the abundant use of Biblical allusions and citations can be explained since, "the Old Testament was, after all, the Bible of those early Christian communities."[6]

It was previously noted that these predominantly Gentile Christian (since it is not possible to rule out the presence of any Jews amongst these communities) converts were described using the word παρεπιδήμοις (1 Pet 1:1). This is repeated in 1 Pet 2:11 in conjunction with the term παροίκους. John H. Elliott's impressive sociological exegesis argues that these terms literally meant that the recipients held the legal status of "exile"/παρεπίδημος and "alien"/πάροικος (or, to use his respective terms, "visitors and resident aliens."[7] Yet, "Elliott's contention that 1 Peter's addressees were non-native residents and visiting strangers . . . is not warranted by the evidence or the first century CE technical use of the words."[8] These terms are in fact both metaphorical and theological. Essentially, they "point to Christians as people who share values other than those of the surrounding world."[9] This reflects the fact that there is some discontent between two groups: the Christian readers and their non-Christian neighbors living together in *politeia*[10] as well as in the private realm of the household. On the latter individualist note, it should be stated that the community comprises slaves (1 Pet 2:18–25), elders (1 Pet 5:1–4), young men (1 Pet 5:5) as well as husbands and wives (1 Pet 3:1–6; 7).[11]

Suffering is a very prominent theme in the First Letter of Peter. Whereas scholars in the past have attended to other motifs within the

6. Achtemeier, *1 Peter*, 51.

7. Elliott, *A Home for the Homeless*, 21.

8. Bechtler, *Following*, 74. Furthermore, Elliot suggests that these two terms designate legal categories. However, if παρεπίδημος equates to "visiting stranger" and πάροικος equates to "resident alien," then Winter's question is an important one: "why is only the former greeted in the opening of the letter and the latter group ignored until both words occur in 2:11?" Winter, *Seek the Welfare of the City*, 16.

9. Achtemeier, *1 Peter*, 82.

10. A first-century term denoting "public life," which "referred to the whole of life in the public domain of a city." Winter, *Seek the Welfare of the City*, 2.

11. That slaves are mentioned without masters may indicate that the readers themselves are not particularly wealthy or affluent.

letter, trends in modern scholarship have understood the importance of this idea in Petrine studies. Including a few possible variant readings, "suffering" is mentioned in 1 Peter on a significant number of occasions. This primary evidence from the Nestle Aland 27th Edition with a brief contextual comment follows in tabular form:

Figure 7: Table of References to Suffering in 1 Peter

	NA27	Context
1:6	ποικίλοις πειρασμοῖς	"Various trials" of readers
1:6	λυπηθέντες	"Having been grieved" by such trials
1:7	δοκιμαζομένου	The faith of readers "being tested"
1:11	τὰ ... παθήματα	"The sufferings" intended for Christ
2:12	καταλαλοῦσιν	Gentiles "speak against" readers as "evildoers"
2:19	ὑποφέρει ... λύπας	Hypothetical pain of slaves ...
2:19	πάσχων	... whilst "suffering"
2:20	κολαφιζόμενοι	Slaves "being beaten"
2:20	πάσχοντες	Slaves "suffering" for doing right
2:21	ἔπαθεν	Christ "suffered" for you
2:23	λοιδορούμενος	Christ did not retaliate whilst "being reviled"
2:23	πάσχων	Christ did not threaten whilst "suffering"
2:23	λοιδορούμενος	Christ did not retaliate whilst "being reviled"
3:9	λοιδορίαν ἀντὶ λοιδορίας	Do not repay "abuse for abuse"
3:14	πάσχοιτε	"if you should suffer ..."
3:14	φόβον αὐτῶν	The readers are not to fear "their fear/terror"
3:16	καταλαλεῖσθε	"You [the readers] are slandered"
3:16	οἱ ἐπηρεάζοντες ὑμῶν	"The ones abusing you [the readers]"
3:17	πάσχειν	It is better "to suffer" for doing right ...
3:18	ἔπαθεν	Christ "suffered" once for all
4:1	παθόντος	Christ "having suffered" in the flesh
4:1	παθὼν	"suffering" in flesh has finished with sin
4:12	πυρώσει	The "fiery ordeal" amongst the readers
4:12	πειρασμὸν	The fiery ordeal is a "test" for the readers
4:13	παθήμασιν	The "sufferings" of Christ
4:14	ὀνειδίζεσθε	If "you [the readers] are reproached ..."

	NA27	Context
4:15	μὴ ... πασχέτω	"Let [no one] suffer" as a murderer ...
4:16	πασχέτω (from 4:15)	... but let that person suffer as a Christian
4:17	τὸ κρίμα	"Judgment" is to begin with the house of God
4:19	οἱ πάσχοντες	"Those suffering" according to the will of God
5:1	παθημάτων	The claims to have seen Christ's "sufferings"
5:9	τῶν παθημάτων	The "sufferings" of the readers' brethren
5:10	παθόντας	After they "have suffered" for a little while

The evidence demonstrates that the various "sufferings" described in the letter are very much associated with two main parties at corresponding locations in time: the past sufferings of Christ and the (definite) present and (likely) future sufferings of the readers. What is required is an attempt to envisage the circumstances of the readers: the form and cause of their sufferings.

From the internal evidence of the letter, it seems quite clear that any reading of 1 Peter must take into consideration the assumption that, "the recipients are being, or at any moment liable to be, subjected to trials and persecutions."[12] Most scholars operate on the assumption that the letter's communities are actually suffering or are imminently threatened with suffering. This best explains 1 Peter's paraenetic activity, for without a genuine context of suffering, the author would be devoid of a rationale for epistolary encouragement: there would be no requirement for a fervent and persuasive case to be made to the addressees. The justifiable premise that the letter's communities are presently suffering is a fundamental insight upon which, so it is claimed, the author introduces a practical theodicy.

Furthermore, to see the way in which 1 Peter works as "theodicy" requires that the text be understood as a genuine letter. Yet historically, a number of scholars have rejected the unity of the letter.[13] These views often prioritize other themes, such as baptism, over-and-above suffering. A frequent redactional claim is that the suffering portrayed within 1 Peter is not uniform or consistent throughout the text. Since different pericopae

---

12. Kelly, *Epistles of Peter and of Jude*, 5.
13. For example, a wide number of thinkers, including F. L. Cross, R. Perdelwitz, H. Preisker, B. H. Streeter, and H. Windisch have argued that 1 Peter should not be read as a genuine letter.

are thought to reflect different descriptions of suffering, this fuels the notion that the letter is indeed not genuine and is instead a matrix of sources. Though these views have generally fallen out of favor, a demonstration of the continuity of suffering within 1 Peter invariably affirms the reasonable claim that 1 Peter is a genuine letter.[14]

All scholars recognize that those in 1 Pet 4:12 and beyond are actual sufferings. However, this has been counterbalanced with the suggestion that the readers' afflictions between 1 Pet 1:3 and 1 Pet 4:11 are only potential. This is twinned with C. F. D. Moule's proposal that, "as there looks to be a distinct break at 4:11 (which records a doxology and an Amen at an apparent close of a letter), we should think of our 1 Peter as made up of two separate compositions," since "in the first the style is calm and measured [as opposed to] a more fearful and nervous atmosphere."[15] However, the textual evidence arguably shows that the sufferings in 1 Pet 1:3–4:11 are not merely potential.

1 Peter 1:6 speaks of ποικίλοις πειρασμοῖς (many trials), denoting the mechanism by which the sufferers "have been affected" (λυπηθέντες, 1 Pet 1:6). The sufferings are spoken of in terms of "tests" or "trials," which fits the context of being refined (1 Pet 1:7).[16] That the refining process is διὰ πυρὸς δοκιμαζομένου (being tested through fire, 1 Pet 1:7) contests Martin's point, since the image is hardly "calm and measured."[17] It has quite the opposite metaphorical impact: it "highlights their severity by likening their effect to the refining action of fire on gold."[18] Moreover, the aorist tense of λυπηθέντες (having been affected, 1 Pet 1:6) without doubt demonstrates that the suffering has already occurred. This is brought out in the NRSV by an indicative verb: "you have had to suffer various trials" (1 Pet 1:6).

The optatives used collectively with εἰ in 1 Pet 3:13–17 might also suggest hypothetical suffering. The writer states εἰ καὶ πάσχοιτε διὰ δικαιοσύνην ("but if you should indeed suffer because of righteousness,"

---

14. In fact, most modern and technical studies of the text have similarly employed this premise. A wide range of scholars, including Achtemeier, Bechtler, Kelly, Troy Martin and Thurén likewise support this assertion.

15. Chester and Martin, *Theology of the Letters of James, Peter and Jude*, 122. See also Moule, *Birth of the New Testament*, 1–11.

16. Bauer, *Lexicon*, 646.

17. Martin, *Theology of the Letters*, 122.

18. Kelly, *1 Peter*, 6.

1 Pet 3:14) and in 1 Pet 3:17 considers it good πάσχειν (to suffer) but only εἰ θέλοι τὸ θέλημα τοῦ θεοῦ (1 Pet 3:17). Grammatically, the optatives do indicate a potential rather than realised state of affairs. However, by no means do they exclude the possibility that suffering is occurring: it simply means that the writer is using theoretical language to made a didactical or instructive point. Furthermore, it is evident from the circumstances previously described in 1 Pet 2:12 ("though they malign you as evildoers . . .") that, "malice and defamation are ever-present realities with which [the] correspondents have to live."[19] From these counter-proofs, it can be justifiably affirmed that considering 1 Pet 4:11 as a partition, should (if at all) be limited to discussion of composition and not to the chronological status of the readers' sufferings.

From this it is plain that the letter as a whole conveys present suffering as the expected reality of life. Yet the forms and nature of these circumstances remains slightly ambiguous. The author often uses very general terms for their suffering as opposed to more technical terms. The primary verb of choice to describe suffering in 1 Peter is πάσχω. Originally, within the works of Homer, it contains the idea of suffering evil. However, thereafter the verb was used to denote the experience of an individual; in that context its nuance included, "everything that befalls a person whether good or ill."[20] However, by the era of the New Testament, the word almost categorically had negative implications yet retained a very general idea of suffering.[21] Within the Greek and Hellenistic world, it generally meant, "having to suffer misfortune, blows of fate, the disfavour of men or gods."[22]

Within the New Testament and other literature,[23] the verb can also have a slightly more specific semantic dimension of "suffering to the end of death." A prime example would be in Luke 22:15, when the verb is used in an articular infinitive construction, indicating that Jesus desired to

19. Ibid., 7.

20. Bauer, *Lexicon*, 639

21. Bauer offers only two possible exceptions to this negative connotation within the NT Canon. Galatians 3:4 seems to require a positive semantic dimension. In Matthew 17:15, Bauer supposes this to have a neutral meaning, although this is further qualified by the unfavourable κακῶς. For further discussion see Bauer, *Lexicon*, 639.

22. Michaelis, "πάσχω," 905.

23. Examples include, Herodian 1, 17,7; Diog. L. 5, 61; Josephus *Ant* 15, 65; 18, 352. For further discussion see Bauer, *Lexicon*, 639; and Michaelis, "πάσχω," 912.

participate in the Passover meal πρὸ τοῦ με παθεῖν (with His disciples before His death). Yet the context of the letter assumes the conventional use of the term. Suffering is considered continuous, for example, in 1 Pet 5:10 (ὀλίγον / a little while, with a sense of consistent endurance). Further, when other verbs are used to describe suffering, the sufferings in view are of various forms (ποικίλοις in 1 Pet 1:6).

Though the meaning of πάσχω is vague, a number of other verbs are used to describe the readers' sufferings. These, in turn, point to vocal (as opposed to physical) attacks upon the Petrine communities. καταλαλέω / "speak against" or "slander" is used twice: as a present indicative active (καταλαλοῦσιν, 1 Pet 2:12) and as a present indicative passive (καταλαλεῖσθε, 1 Pet 3:16). In addition, there are a handful of other terms in the letter: ἐπηρεάζω (1 Pet 3:16) meaning "abusing" with a vocal threatening force;[24] ὀνειδίζω/"reproaching" (1 Pet 4:14) and λοιδορέω/"reviling" (1 Pet 2:23; 3:19). From these, it is plausible that the writer could have meant to indicate "the rough justice of unofficial accusation."[25]

Though these terms point to local persecutions, some within the history of Petrine scholarship have wished to view State persecution as the source of the communities' sufferings. Two phrases in the letter are important. That the readers would be under threat for ὀνόματι Χριστοῦ (1 Pet 4:14) in addition to ὡς Χριστιανός (1 Pet 4:16) have been interpreted by some scholars as support for this assumption. Admittedly, ἐν ὀνόματι Χριστοῦ (1 Pet 4:14) bears a striking resemblance to the persecutions mentioned by Pliny the Younger in his letter to Trajan (98–117 CE), enquiring, "whether Christians should be punished for bearing 'the name itself'"[26] or only if they are guilty of other crimes as well."[27] Moreover, a specific state persecution was undertaken by Pliny in the region of Bithynia, one of the provinces of Asia Minor to which 1 Peter is addressed. Before this time, the earliest known persecution in these Eastern regions of the Empire was under Domitian (93–96 CE).

This becomes all the more complicated when considering the dating of the letter. Most reasonable suggestions of a date for the letter's composition propose a time some years earlier. Certainly an upper boundary for

---

24. Attested by Bauer, *Lexicon*, 285.
25. Moule, *Birth*, 113.
26. Pliny *Letters* X.96
27. Johnson, *Writings of the New Testament*, 482.

the date would 130 CE, since the work is cited by Polycarp in his Letter to the Philippians (ca. 135 CE) and, according to Eusebius,[28] by Papias of Hierapolis (60 CE—130 CE). More conservative scholars, who assert an authentic Petrine authorship, conclude that it must have been written before the persecutions in Rome, probably in the early 60s CE and appeal to the author's claim to have been a "witness of the sufferings of Christ" (1 Pet 5:1). However, the honest approach admits that the evidence is totally inconclusive.

Yet all this should not detract from the fact that the letter *in toto* does not really fit neatly into a model of State persecution. I would suggest a number of key reasons in support of this statement: the terminology used to advocate "State persecutions" does not necessarily contain that connotation; the earliest Gospel even mentions suffering "for the name" in Mark 8:13. This term simply denoted a common Christian experience, admittedly taken up at a later stage by State authorities. In fact the term "state persecution" itself is indeed a thorny one, most of the evidence available for this period suggest that "there was no general Roman policy regarding Christians";[29] Achtemeier has shown that, though Christians were indeed persecuted under Domitian's reign (not only for a general distrust of *collegia*,[30] but for resistance to the Emperor's title as *deus et dominus noster*),[31] the persecution was relatively "spasmodic and lacked the kind of organization that would allow it to be labelled 'official persecution.'"[32]

Nor can the theory of state persecution be supported from a peculiar reading of 1 Pet 3:15, in which a formal hearing before a magistrate is envisioned. ἀπολογία/"defence" (1 Pet 3:15) does indeed have a judicial feel as does λόγος/"account" (1 Pet 3:15).[33] If anything, this would indicate that the community's persecution was endorsed, not by Imperial order, but officially by local legal authorities.[34] However, neither is appar-

---

28. Eusebius *Ecclesiastical History* 3.39.17.

29. Achtemeier, *1 Peter*, 33.

30. *Collegia* or "organised groups" were often feared by Emperors as, "secret organisations pursuing political interests (*hetareiae*)," Achtemeier, *1 Peter*, 26.

31. The title translates as "our god and lord", a customary address for Domitian according to Seutonius *Vit.* 8.13.2.

32. Achtemeier, *1 Peter*, 32.

33. ἀπολογία is used of a legal defence in Acts 25:16; 26:2; and 2 Tim 4:16.

34. "The principal legal basis of such persecution appears to have been the procedure of *coercitio* that local authorities had at their disposal, and that allowed them, at their own

ent, since the author state that the account must be given to "anyone who demands from you an account of the hope that is in you" (1 Pet 3:15). Far from the feared or detested source of persecution (as some readings have it), the authority and operation of state and judicial powers are described to work in accordance with the Divine will and standards.

It should further be noted that the attitude presented within the letter towards state authority is generally positive. Speaking of the civic disciplinary practices of the day, in 1 Pet 2:14–15, "the role of the governing authority in punishing crime is referred to with obvious approval."[35] In fact, these judicial authorities are "God's agent to reward good behavior and punish bad behavior."[36] This much is obvious from the fact that the authorities are said to be: ὡς δι' αὐτοῦ πεμπομένοις εἰς ἐκδίκησιν (1 Pet 2:14). In fact, the entire pericope of 1 Pet 2:13–17 advocates a "quietist" or "conformist" attitude towards state authorities. The author begins with the passive aorist imperative: ὑποτάγητε (1 Pet 2:13). The emphasis is thus on the necessity to be subject to human institutions, whether of the Emperor (1 Pet 2:14; 17) or the more local Governor (1 Pet 2:14). The word, "king" in Greek, was applicable to most "client princes" whom Rome allowed to rule in certain provinces, such as in Egypt, Palestine, and Syria, but belonged "par excellence"[37] to the Emperor. The Roman Emperor is given a supreme earthly place in this letter, and spoken of in a positive light: the author commands, ". . . honor the Emperor" (1 Pet 2:17).

Additionally, the predominant vocabulary used by the author (in addition to πάσχω) contains the idea of mainly verbal and not physical attacks and, lastly, much of the internal evidence of the letter includes other reasons (e.g., Christian behavior) as the reason for the Christians' sufferings. These last two assertions themselves point to unofficial local persecutions ("bottom up") rather than organized official state and/or local "top down" persecutions.

Johnson believes that, "the author's depiction of the believers' suffering points to a context of social ostracism."[38] Surely such a statement is misleading, for it implies that the active party performing the exclusion

discretion, to decree and enforce policies intended to maintain public order," Achtemeier, *1 Peter*, 34.

35. Marshall, *Beyond Retribution*, 147.
36. Ibid., 198.
37. Kelly, *1 Peter*, 107.
38. Johnson, *Writings*, 483.

are the non-Christian neighbors. However, the reverse would seem to me to be the case: the believers are being vilified because they have, in some way, withdrawn themselves from *politeia*. In addition to mentioning the hostility of the non-Christian neighbors, the author describes them as ignorant (1 Pet 2:15) and suspicious (1 Pet 2:12; 4:14–16). The public reaction is likely to be rooted in the Christians', "breaking of social bonds, and the cultic ties which they entailed," which "prompted not only a sense of estrangement on the part of the deserted cronies but also their angry denunciation of the Christians as well as their God."[39]

When converting to Christianity and taking upon themselves the common identity of the Christian communities of Asia Minor, these individuals, "ceased participating in certain social activities that they deemed inappropriate and, ultimately, idolatrous."[40] Though Roman tolerance towards other customs was generally tolerated, ancestry and heritage were paramount to value placed upon religious practices.[41] Christianity, if anything, would have been considered *collegia* into which the community have withdrawn. Therefore, "it is not surprising that such 'conspicuous non-participation' in public life was viewed by the larger society as profoundly antisocial behavior."[42]

Modern scholars, theologians and anthropologists together, have recognised the importance of honour and shame in the Mediterranean world. Peculiar withdrawal from *politeia*, in terms of the breaking of social ties and the termination of practices, could be perceived as shameful behaviour. Within the letter, the δοξ- (1 Pet 1:8; 2:12; 4:11; 4:14; 4:16) and the τιμ- (1 Pet 1:7; 2:17; 3:7) word groups of the honour semantic field are mentioned a total of twenty times. There exists an emphatic stress to act honourably: not only towards individuals, such as the βασιλέα (1 Pet 2:17) and γυναῖκες (1 Pet 3:7, referring to 3:1), but also generally towards πάντας (1 Pet 2:17). As Eve puts it, "Honour, a pivotal value in Mediterranean society, is precisely what these Christians lack in the eyes of their unbelieving neighbours."[43] The essential dilemma of the suffering community, and indeed the source of their injustices, is then, "the perva-

---

39. Elliott, *A Home for the Homeless*, 80. Elliott's comments on this matter of social conflict are far less contestable than his claims about παρεπίδημος and πάροικος.

40. Bechtler, *Following*, 83–84.

41. For further discussion, see Achtemeier, *1 Peter*, 24

42. Bechtler, *Following*, 84.

43. Eve, "1 Peter," 1266.

sive threat to their honor inherent in their daily social intercourse with the larger society."[44]

This part of the paper has expounded the readers' situation, one epitomized by suffering. In addition to finding a general location and composition of the Petrine communities, comment has been made concerning the actual sufferings of the recipients. This suffering is likely not in the form of Imperial persecution, but on the local or "grass roots" level within non-Christian Gentile communities in Asia Minor. The hostilities are probably vocal, since the idea of "suffering to the point of death" does not sit well within the context of the letter. As believers became Christians (not necessarily a shameful act in itself), the nature of the Christians' behavior within *politeia* changed, bringing their honor into question. The Petrine communities resultantly face enmity.

THE BEGINNINGS OF THEODICY

Yet this disturbing social problem mutates into a profound theological problem, when taken alongside the traditional Judaeo-Christian ethical portrait of God. Theodicy is concerned etymologically with the vindication of the divine attributes (from θεός and δίκη). Though 1 Peter does not explicitly state it propositionally, it is certainly fair to claim that the letter understands God to be morally "righteous." 1 Peter states that God is holy (1:16); One to be feared as the emperor is honored (2:17); a just judge (2:18–20, 4:5); One who blesses (3:9); One who favors the righteous and who turns His face from evil (3:12); patient (3:20); linked with a good conscience (3:21), One who bestows grace (4:10) and a faithful Creator (4:19). If God is so faithful, then why do the communities suffer?

To resolve the paradox, the author begins by appealing to Divine providence. 1 Peter considers the suffering of the community as that which is happening κατὰ τὸ θέλημα τοῦ θεοῦ (1 Pet 4:19). θέλημα can be used objectively (to describe what is willed) or subjectively (the act of willing, in this case primarily associated with God). Bauer considers 1 Pet 2:15 as an example of the objective use of the noun, and 1 Pet 3:17 and 4:19 as subjective examples.[45] The subjective application of the noun is most relevant here. From the employment of the conditional particle

---

44. Bechtler, *Following*, 20.
45. Bauer, *Lexicon*, 354–55.

εἰ, 1 Pet 3:17 seems to imply that suffering is by no means an absolutely necessary desire of the will of God.

Yet, in the communities' instance, suffering is the will of God (1 Pet 4:19). The author does state that the period of suffering is, thankfully, ὀλίγον, or "for a short duration of time" (1 Pet 1:5; 5:10). What is more, this "negative" piece of paraenesis (encouragement that endeavors to tame the experience of suffering in the readers' minds) is further offset with a beatific futurist vision of eternal inheritance (1 Pet 1:4).[46] Suffering is therefore bound up with the temporal period directly preceding the future epoch and, resultantly, is related to the Christian quality of this expectant temporal phase: faith. As such, it is of more worth than anything of earthly fiscal value, such as gold (1 Pet 1:7). The purpose clause of 1 Pet 1:7 further explains that the communities' faith under duress is linked to Christ's coming glory, which, in turn, reveals the ultimate purpose of faith in 1 Pet 1:9: the salvation of their souls.

Concerning the future inheritance of 1 Pet 1:4, κληρονομία/ "inheritance" is used plentifully in the LXX.[47] Though the term can mean literal "possessions" (indeed, for the Hebrew people this possession represented the land of Canaan)[48] it is used in the Septuagint to denote things other than material possession.[49] Within early Christian usage it took on a more eschatological nuance as the "kingdom."[50] In its Petrine context, it complements the language of rebirth in 1 Pet 1:3, such that the regenerated people become heirs of God's inheritance, which is eternal life. This is made clear from the fact that σωτηρίαν (1 Pet 1:5), a term used in Judaism to signify deliverance from God's final judgment, is actually grammatically dependent upon τετηρημένην (1 Pet 1:4). This inheritance is kept ἐν οὐρανοῖς εἰς ὑμᾶς (1 Pet 1:4) and, on account of its logical identity with

---

46. The fact that scholars have suggested that 1 Pet 1:3–4 may be comprised of a liturgical source in no way detracts from this vision: the writer positively includes this source and (according to these adherents) actually adds his own material to expand the thought (so Kelly, *1 Peter*, 52).

47. Skaggs, *Pentecostal Commentary on 1 Peter, 2 Peter and Jude*, 18. According to her, it is used in the LXX over 200 times.

48. For example, in Deut 15:4 and 19:10.

49. In Pss 16:5 and 73:25 it is used of God Himself; in Dan 12:13 it describes eternal life.

50. The noun is used in a parable of Jesus (Matt 21:38//Mark 12:7//Luke 20:14) and, more pertinently, the verbal form is used in Matt 25:34//Mark 10:17//Luke 10:25.

σωτηρίαν, the inheritance is ἑτοίμην ἀποκαλυφθῆναι ἐν καιρῷ ἐσχάτῳ (1 Pet 1:5).

Thereupon, the author then states ἐν ᾧ ἀγαλλιᾶσθε (1 Pet 1:6). This phrase is riddled with various textual and syntactical difficulties. Firstly, the relative pronoun could either take a masculine or neuter referent. If masculine, it could refer to Χριστοῦ (1 Pet 1:3), θεοῦ (1 Pet 1:5) or καιρῷ (1 Pet 1:5). However, it is more likely that the pronoun be read as neuter,[51] such that, "the antecedent would be the content of the previous verses, finding in that the reason for rejoicing despite the unfavourable circumstances."[52] Secondly, the mood of ἀγαλλιᾶσθε could be imperative or indicative. However, in any case, it is quite clear from the context of the verse that the writer considers an attitude of "joy throughout suffering" (whether exhorted or simply described) on account of the certainty of the future sequence of events. In this way, the overwhelming joy of the future to come should, for the readers, far outweigh the present experience of passing suffering, already diminishing (ὀλίγον) in impetus. The futurist emphasis is continued by the author later in the letter with the command to τελείως ἐλπίσατε (1 Pet 1:13).

Yet the author's ideas concerning duration and future inheritance do not conclude the matter entirely; for he has only gone as far as demonstrating that God's plans for the community are, in this case, good. The author must then demonstrate, contra an arbitrary understanding of God's will, how God's action is universally good: that His plans are trustworthy everywhere and always. In other words, the "suffering prior to future glory" motif itself must still be reconciled with God's character. As a matter of fact, the author does indeed accomplish this by means of drawing the experiences of the recipients into a Christological narrative.

The addressees are reminded of the fact that God remains their πιστῷ κτίστῃ (1 Pet 4:19). Herein lies a clue to the solution. That "Creator" (as a noun, not a participle) is *hapax legomenon* is a fact widely discussed amongst the commentaries. The pericope is one of divine judgment and Michaels claims that, "God's authority as universal judge rest[s] on his role as creator of all people."[53] This universal statement does not, however,

---

51. Additionally, if it were masculine and referred to καιρῷ, then ἀγαλλιᾶσθε would have to be understood as a verb in the future tense; a difficult reading of a present tense verb.

52. Achtemeier, *1 Peter*, 100.

53. Michaels, *1 Peter*, 274.

exclude the precise theological idea that God Himself is, quite literally, the creator of the early Christian community. The identity of the Petrine recipients has been established κατὰ πρόγνωσιν θεοῦ (1 Pet 1:2). This, however, is not a detached knowledge, but one that dependent upon God's own volitional creative act, since the correspondents are themselves depicted adjectivally as ἐκλεκτοῖς / "chosen" (1 Pet 1:1).

Thereupon the parallelism between the suffering of the addressees and the letter's Christology and atonement theology is striking. For just as the forging of the community as well as their present suffering was instantiated by a faithful God's will, Christ's sufferings were also brought about by the operation of the Divine will. 1 Pet 1:11 speaks of Christ's sufferings as προμαρτυρόμενον, another word prefixed with "fore-"/ προ-. Moreover, the fact that the community's existence stands in relation to the atoning act of Christ is underscored by the affinity with the "sprinkling" of Christ's blood in 1 Pet 1:2. The theodicy then comes full circle, for God's will did not only predestine sufferings for Christ, but His "subsequent glory" (1 Pet 1:11), namely "his resurrection, ascension, enthronement on high . . . and, not least, His final 'revelation.'"[54] Christ's act, whilst playing the pivotal function in the formation of the community itself, becomes simultaneously a model and inspiration to the letter's recipients.

CONCLUSION

To summarize, the structure of my understanding of 1 Peter's theodicy as a point of coherence between the addressees and the atonement theology is as follows: the author demonstrates how the eschatologically blessed future compensates, and indeed prevails over, the affliction of the present. God's goodness is demonstrated by the positive establishment of this early Church community, which proceeds directly from Christ's atoning act. Similarly, Christ's own suffering was part of God's plan, whose proclaimed glory is comparable to the addressees' future inheritance. All this occurs within the operation of their faithful God's will: a will that volitionally instantiates the community's future inheritance, present sufferings and, similarly, the sufferings of their Savior.

Having expounded the theodicy, comment should be made regarding the challenges of this methodology. It would seem that there are two distinct, yet related, questions to ask. Firstly, is it appropriate to use this

54. Kelly, *1 Peter*, 61.

systematic idea in reference to an *ad hoc* epistolary text? I believe that it is. On the justifiable assumption that 1 Peter is a genuine letter, theodicy certainly facilitates a better understanding of its function. It affirms what conventional wisdom already tells us: that suffering is pre-eminently the most important theme of the letter: it is related to its recipients' situation as well as to other aspects, such as atonement theology and ethics.

Furthermore, theodicy rightly acknowledges the paraenetic function of the letter, but also supplements this exhortation with a positive expression of the goodness of God: an idea doubtlessly brought into question by the circumstances of the Petrine communities. Far from retrojecting a concept back onto an ancient work, this idea elucidates the earliest reception of the text and the theology of the letter.

Secondly, in what way is it a theodicy? The letter is plainly not a *magnum opus* of philosophical theology. Yet it should be noted that "theodicy" is a technical expression that has been hijacked by philosophers of religion to wrestle with the so-called "inconsistent triad": God's omnipotence, God's omnibenevolence and the reality of the existence of evil. Put more simply, however, it amounts to a way of expressing the righteousness or goodness of God in the light of apparent evidence to the contrary. Without doubt, this is most apt to the aims and purpose of 1 Peter. Just as the moral injunctions of the New Testament are to normative ethical theories, and as the various theological and Christological pericopes of the Biblical texts are to a doctrine of God, so this Petrine proto-theodicy stands in relation to the later traditions of theodicy.

BIBLIOGRAPHY

Achtemeier, Paul J. *1 Peter*. Hermeneia. Minneapolis: Fortress, 1996.
Bauckham, Richard. "James, 1 Peter, Jude and 2 Peter." In *A Vision for the Church*, edited by M. Bockmuehl and M. B. Thompson, 153–66. Edinburgh: T. & T. Clark, 1997.
Bauer, Walter. *A Greek-English Lexicon*. Translated by W. F. Arndt and F. W. Gingrich. Chicago: University of Chicago Press, 1957.
Brox, Norbert. *Der erste Petrusbrief*. 3rd ed. Evangelisch-Katholisches Kommentar zum Neuen Testament 21. Zurich: Benziger, 1989.
Beare, Francis Wright. *The First Epistle of Peter*. 3rd ed. Oxford: Blackwell, 1970.
Bechtler, Stephen Richard. *Following in His Steps: Suffering, Community and Christology in 1 Peter*. SBL Dissertation Series 162. Atlanta: Scholars, 1998.
Chester, Andrew, and Ralph P. Martin, editors. *Theology of the Letters of James, Peter and Jude*. New Testament Theology. Cambridge: Cambridge University Press, 1994.
Elliott, John H. *A Home for the Homeless: A Social-scientific Criticism of I Peter, Its Situation and Strategy*. 1990. Reprinted, Eugene, OR: Wipf & Stock, 2005.
Eve, Eric. "1 Peter." In *The Oxford Bible Commentary*, edited by John Barton and John Muddiman, 1263–69. Oxford: Oxford University Press, 2001.
Fredosso, Alfred J., translator. *On Divine Foreknowledge (Molina's Concordia)*. London: Cornell University Press, 1988.
Johnson, Luke Timothy. *The Writings of the New Testament: An Interpretation*. Rev. ed. Minneapolis: Fortress, 1999.
Kelly, J. N. D. *A Commentary on the Epistles of Peter and of Jude*. Black's New Testament Commentaries. London: A. & C. Black, 1969.
Lohse, Eduard. "Parenesis and Kerygma in 1 Peter." In *Perspectives on First Peter*, edited by Charles H. Talbert, 37–59. Macon, GA: Mercer University Press, 1986.
Marshall, Christopher D. *Beyond Retribution: A New Testament Vision for Justice, Crime, and Punishment*. Studies in Peace and Scripture. Grand Rapids: Eerdmans, 2001.
Martin, Troy W. *Metaphor and Composition in 1 Peter*. SBL Dissertation Series 131. Atlanta: Scholars, 1992.
Michaels, J. Ramsey. *1 Peter*. Word Biblical Commentary. Waco, TX: Word, 1999.
Michaelis, Wilhelm. "πάσχω." In *Theological Dictionary of the New Testament*, edited by Gerhard Friedrich, 5:904–24. Translated by Geoffrey W. Bromiley. Grand Rapids: Eerdmans, 1968.
Millauer, Helmut. *Leiden als Gnade: Eine traditionsgeshichtlich Untersuchung zur Leidenstheologie des erstens Petrusbriefes*. Europäisches Hochschulschriften 23.56. Bern: Lang, 1976.
Moule, C. F. D. *The Birth of the New Testament*. London: A. & C. Black, 1966.
Selwyn, Edward Gordon. *The First Epistle of St. Peter*. London: Macmillan, 1964.
Skaggs, Rebecca. *Pentecostal Commentary on 1 Peter, 2 Peter, Jude*. Pentecostal Commentary: New Testament. London: T. & T. Clark, 2004.
Thurén, Lauri. *Argument and Theology in 1 Peter*. JSNTSS 114. Sheffield: Sheffield Academic, 2002.
Winter, Bruce W. *Seek the Welfare of the City: Christians as Benefactors and Citizens*. First-Century Christians in the Graeco-Roman World. Grand Rapids: Eerdmans, 1994.

9

Interpreting Together and Receiving New Testament Concepts of Apostolicity

Miriam Haar

FEW SECONDARY PUBLICATIONS EXIST on the topic of interpretation and reception of the New Testament term "apostle," or the notions of "apostolic," "apostolate" and "apostolicity" in ecumenical statements. Thus, a researcher might widen his scope to biblical concepts in ecumenical documents and related areas. But again, what exists is far from satisfying. There are, however, an abundance of publications on questions like "Who were the Apostles?," written by scholars of Biblical Studies,[1] as well as a huge number of publications on the contentious issue of the Apostolicity of the Church written by scholars of Ecumenical Theology, mainly systematic theologians.[2] In addition, there are a great variety of publications on hermeneutics, interpretation and reception.[3] In summation, very little scholarly work exists on the intersection of the fields of Biblical Studies and Ecumenical Studies. Therefore, this paper seeks to encourage interdisciplinary discussion.

The focus of this paper is first on the debate over the Apostolicity of the Christian Church. The second section examines the usage of the terms ἀποστέλλειν ("to send") and ἀπόστολος ("someone who has been sent") in Greek language, as well as the usage of שלח ("send"), the cor-

---

1. E.g., Frey, "Apostelbegriff, Apostelamt und Apostolizität."

2. E.g., Burkhard, *Apostolicity Then and Now*.

3. E.g., Gaventa, "Interpreting Scriptures Together; Tetley, "Use of the Bible in Ecumenical Dialogue involving Anglicans."

responding Hebrew term. The third section critically analyzes how these biblical notions are interpreted and received in the ecumenical statement *The Apostolicity of the Church* (2006) and asks whether their complexity is reflected in that document. Finally, this paper offers suggestions for further reflection on the interpretation and reception of biblical concepts in ecumenical documents.

APOSTOLICITY AS A CENTRAL TOPIC OF ECUMENICAL RESEARCH

According to the Nicene-Constantinopolitan Creed (381 CE), Christian believers adhere to the notion of the Church as one, holy, catholic, and apostolic. However, the churches still do not agree on the meaning of the last of the so-called "four marks" or attributes of the Church. Apostolicity remains one of the most divisive issues between churches. Only a rather minimalistic definition of apostolicity, by which the churches understand their continued faithful existence in the Christian tradition of the apostles, is shared by all Christian churches. Therefore, apostolicity is one of the most contested issues in ecumenical theology, and an important, if not the *most* important, aspect of the ongoing process to develop an ecumenical ecclesiology (that is, an understanding of the Church shared by all the Christian churches in dialogue).

Apostolicity is indispensable for the understanding of ordained ministry, episcopé, episcopacy, apostolic succession, the role of papacy, etc. Furthermore, a variety of topics (such as the question of authority or the understanding of tradition) which are also relevant for the development of an ecumenical ecclesiology are explicitly or implicitly linked to apostolicity. As the term "apostolic" relates to the self-understanding of the churches, a shared understanding of the Church cannot be reached without further agreement on the meaning of apostolicity.

For many churches, apostolicity has been a crucial topic in the history of the Church and its doctrine, and was used in apologetics as a touchstone to prove a church's authenticity. One approach to apostolicity perceives continuity in a linear, person-centered way, which is preserved in some church traditions, and other church traditions are therefore seen in a state of discontinuity. This is especially problematic when the recognition of a church tradition as a Church hinges on such an understanding. Those churches who are denied apostolicity claim this mark of the

Church for themselves—though based on a different rationale. Because of the enormous impact these different understandings of apostolicity have, determining the meaning of apostolicity has been an unavoidable problem since the beginning of the modern ecumenical movement. Although in its early history the issue of apostolicity was not an explicit focal point, it recurred regularly in debates on the Tradition of the Church, its four marks, apostolic succession, episcopacy, etc. Few attempts were made to gain a shared foundation, beyond the fact that all churches ascribe some normativity to the apostles and that the apostolic age was decisive in the shaping of the Church. Apostolicity only came to the fore at the Fourth General Assembly of the World Council of Churches at Uppsala in 1968. Since then, apostolicity has been a crucial topic in ecumenical dialogue; nearly every dialogue addressed apostolicity in one way or another. One of the most recent documents concerning apostolicity is the Roman Catholic-Lutheran document *The Apostolicity of the Church*. Before looking at this document, the biblical foundations[4] of the semantic field "apostle" must be examined in order to establish a basis from which the interpretation and reception of these terms in more recent ecumenical statements can be critically analyzed.

CONCEPTS OF APOSTOLICITY IN BIBLICAL SCRIPTURES

When examining concepts of apostolicity in biblical scriptures, the emphasis must be on the exegetical discussion and the results of historical-critical research. The complexity of the biblical scriptures must be considered in order to avoid the suspicion of ideological construction, which supports controversies instead of helping to solve them. Although it may seem obvious, is must be reiterated at the beginning of this chapter that the adjective "apostolic" as an attribute of the Church or as a description of a certain doctrine or the right constitution of the Church does not occur in the New Testament. The use of the adjective "apostolic"

---

4. Although extracanonical scriptures offer important insights to the understanding of "apostle," they are not in the center of attention in this paper, because the examined ecumenical documents focus mainly on scriptures within the biblical canon. It must be noted that the question, "Which scriptures are included in the biblical canon?" is also an issue in ecumenical dialogue as significant, but not full agreement on the biblical canon has been reached (e.g., the reflections on the Canon, Scripture and Tradition as well as the Church's teaching office, in *The Apostolicity of the Church*, §§390–428).

comes relatively late, and the New Testament only talks of the apostles as persons.

Answering the question "Who were the apostles?" is complicated. The Greek word ἀπόστολος, from which the English word "apostle" comes, is derived from the verb ἀποστέλλειν, first as a verbal adjective and then as a noun. The verb ἀποστέλλειν is a compound of στέλλειν, "to put up, make ready" and the preposition ἀπό, "from, away, back," and means "send (both person and things), send away, chase away [and], send off." In classical Greek literature ἀπόστολος is first found in maritime language, where it means a "naval ship," a "cargo ship," or "the fleet sent out," and, in later literature, "a delegate" or "a messenger." All its usages have two ideas in common: Firstly, they express commission, and secondly, being sent overseas.

Some scholars stress that there is no parallel in classical Greek to the religious use of the word.[5] However, others argue that, e.g., in Gnostic circles ἀπόστολος came to convey the oriental concept of emissaries as mediators of divine revelation.[6]

In Judaism the corresponding Aramaic word שלח was a title given to men sent from Jerusalem to Jewish communities abroad. This may have influenced the Christian use of the word. However, the roots of the New Testament term lay in the Hebrew Bible and Judaism, in which משלח (passive participle of שלח) played an important role. In the Hebrew Bible and Jewish Tradition, a legal convention existed according to which the delegate represents the one who has sent him (cf. mBer 5:5). This understanding stands behind, e.g., the sending out of the disciples in Luke 10:16, "Whoever listens to you listens to me, and whoever rejects you rejects me, and whoever rejects me rejects the one who sent me" (Cf. 2 Cor 5:20). Usually the authorization is limited, but שלח is understood to connote lifelong sending (e.g., Isa 6:8): "Then I heard the voice of the Lord saying, 'Whom shall I send, and who will go for us?' And I said, 'Here am I; send me!'"

Accordingly, the New Testament talks of the sending of the prophets (e.g., Luke 4:26: "yet Elijah was sent to none of them except to a widow at Zarephath in Sidon.") or John the Baptist (e.g., Mark 1:2: "As it is written in the prophet Isaiah, "See, I am sending my messenger ahead of you,

---

5. Cf. Kertelge, "Apostel."
6. Cf. ibid.

who will prepare your way.'") This is also presupposed for the sending of Jesus, as described, e.g., in Gal 4:4: "But when the fullness of time had come, God sent his Son."[7] The connection of constant authorization and proclamation of the gospel which is constitutive for the understanding of an apostle is given by Isa 61:1, "The Spirit of the Sovereign Lord is on me, because the Lord has anointed me to preach good news to the poor. He has sent me to bind up the broken-hearted, to proclaim freedom for the captives and release from darkness for the prisoners . . ." and explicitly taken over in Luke 4:16–21 (cf. 1:19) where it is described that Jesus went into the Synagogue on the Sabbath day and read exactly these sentences from the prophet Isaiah.

However, the New Testament, which uses the verb ἀποστέλλειν 131 times, features different understandings of the term ἀπόστολος.[8] In general, it means "envoy, ambassador, apostle." In contrast to the Septuagint (LXX), the frequent occurrence of the noun ἀπόστολος in the New Testament is something new. In the Pauline epistles, which are regarded as the oldest source of information about the technical use of ἀπόστολος in the New Testament, we find ἀπόστολοι ἐκκλεσιόν who only have a limited mission by congregations (e.g., 2 Cor 8:23), ἀπόστολοι Ἰησοῦ Χριστοῦ who are appointed by Christ, and ἀπόστολοι ὑπερλίαν who are regarded as pseudo-apostles (e.g., 2 Cor 11:5. 13).

The first written evidence of ἀπόστολος in the New Testament is derived from a pre-Pauline creedal formula that Paul has incorporated in his first letter to the Corinthians (1 Cor 15:3–7).[9] After the creedal formula, Paul continues by speaking of his own experience of the risen Lord and of his calling to apostleship (1 Cor 15:8–11). 1 Cor 15 reveals two groups (and three, if one includes the five hundred brethren) of witnesses to the risen Lord. There was the group of Twelve and a group of apostles, both of which might evoke the שלח concept.[10] As such, a distinction between the

---

7. E.g., Rom 8:3; John 3:17, etc.; cf. also the term "apostle" in Heb 3:1.

8. Cf. Hahn. "Apostel. I. Neues Testament"; Roloff, "Apostel/Apostolat/Apostolizität."

9. 1 Cor 15:3–7: "3For I handed on to you as of first importance what I in turn had received: that Christ died for our sins in accordance with the scriptures, 4and that he was buried, and that he was raised on the third day in accordance with the scriptures, 5and that he appeared to Cephas, then to the twelve. 6Then he appeared to more than five hundred brothers and sisters at one time, most of whom are still alive, though some have died. 7Then he appeared to James, then to all the apostles."

10. John P. Meier has discussed 1 Cor 15:3–7 at some length in "The Circle of the Twelve," particularly in 659–63. He stresses the historicity of the group of Twelve dur-

Twelve and the apostles can be concluded. Luke uses ἀπόστολος expressly for the twelve, and never calls Paul an apostle. It is remarkable that such a fundamental concept only appears once in each of the other three gospels (cf. John 13:16; Matt 10:2; Mark 6:30). Likewise, these three gospels do not use the expression apostle for the twelve.[11] Paul seems to know a wider circle of apostles (e.g., Rom 16:7).[12] We can identify some of these earliest apostles by pointing out that they received a resurrection appearance of the Lord, e.g., James, the brother of the Lord (e.g., 1 Cor 15:7; Gal 19).[13]

The development of the notion of "apostle" does not end with Paul and Luke. There is a trajectory of images defining "apostle" well into the second century. Thus, we can distinguish between original apostles and a late first-century category of apostles. The notion of apostle and apostolate as well as and the identification of the Twelve with the apostles all came about post Easter. After the time of Paul, when the Twelve became increasingly regarded as the only legitimate bearers of the message of Jesus as the Christ, and the conviction that they had been the initiators of the mission to the Gentiles became generally accepted, the title of apostle was gradually transferred to the whole circle of the Twelve (cf. the list of names in Matt 10:2–3; Mark 3:16–18; Luke 6:13–16 and Acts 1:13, which are not totally congruent). From a certain point in history, the apostles were seen as genuine representatives of authentic doctrine and prototypical representatives of the ecclesial office.[14]

---

ing the ministry of Jesus and concentrates on the eschatological symbolism of their number.

11. The best general introduction on the notion of the apostles is still Roloff, "Apostel/Apostolat/Apostolizität."

12. Cf. Rudolf Schnackenburg who speaks of a pre-Pauline understanding of apostles, an understanding that includes a larger number of individuals than is usually assumed (Schnackenburg, "Apostles before and during Paul's Time"; Schnackenburg, "Apostolicity—The Present Position of Studies."

13. But many others are referred to as "apostles" without any indication as to whether they met certain criteria presumed by the earliest community. John J. Burkhard, e.g., argues that far more than sixteen such people were called "apostles" (cf. Burkhard, *Apostolicity Then and Now*, 10); cf. Roloff, "Apostel/Apostolat/Apostolizität," 432–33.

14. Cf. Wenz, "Von Aposteln und apostolischer Nachfolge."

THE APOSTOLICITY OF THE CHURCH: STUDY DOCUMENT OF THE LUTHERAN-ROMAN CATHOLIC COMMISSION ON UNITY

After having examined the biblical foundation of apostolicity, this chapter critically analyzes the interpretation and reception of ἀποστέλλειν and ἀπόστολος in a recent ecumenical statement and asks whether the complexity of their usage is reflected in this document. Because of the large number of ecumenical documents which deal with apostolicity, either explicitly or implicitly, it is not possible to integrate all findings. The focus is on the study document *The Apostolicity of the Church* by the Pontifical Council for Promoting Christian Unity and the Lutheran World Federation of 2006, not only because it is one of the most recent and extensive studies dedicated to apostolicity, but also because Roman-Catholic–Lutheran Dialogue is a dialogue between churches that share a history in which theological controversy on apostolicity has played an important role. This is arguably the dialogue that has progressed furthest. In post-Reformation times, the debate on apostolicity was mostly limited to the contentious tenet of apostolic succession. From its earliest document, the *Malta Report* (1972),[15] the dialogue between these two church traditions repeatedly addressed matters pertaining to Apostolicity. *The Ministry in the Church* (1981) and *Church and Justification* (1994)[16] perceived future debate on Apostolicity, more specifically under the perspective of ministry in an ecclesiological context, as a way forward to build on agreement on justification and to elucidate implications of such an agreement. The result of a subsequent study process from 1995-2006, which was initiated even prior to the *Joint Declaration on the Doctrine of Justification*, was published in *The Apostolicity of the Church*.

This study document is divided into four parts. Part 1 offers a careful examination of New Testament texts pertaining to the apostles and the main aspects of apostolicity. The document then sets forth the outcome of investigations from three specific perspectives on apostolicity, namely apostolicity as a creedal attribute of the church in Part 2, as a characteristic of church ministry in Part 3, and as a decisive quality of the teachers and doctrine which our churches require in order to remain in the truth of the gospel in Part 4. The commission hopes that the study will open

---

15. Cf. "Malta Report," in *Growth in Agreement*.
16. Cf. "Church and Justification," in *Growth in Agreement II*.

"fresh perspectives in the area of ecumenical ecclesiology and will throw light on pathways along which significant steps may be taken toward the goal of full communion between the Catholic Church and the Lutheran churches of the world."[17]

It is evident in each part of the document that this text is firmly rooted in the Bible, as each part starts with a "Biblical Orientation," and, as references to biblical texts are made frequently throughout the entire document. As the introductory "Biblical Orientations" in the subsequent parts repeat, to some extent, what has already been said in detail in the first part of the document, this paper examines Part 1, "The Apostolicity of the Church—New Testament Foundations," in detail and only makes where it proves to be beneficial a few observations on the subsequent parts. Although this document pays more attention to Scripture, and its interpretation, than other ecumenical documents on the Apostolicity of the Church do, the first part "The Apostolicity of the Church—New Testament Foundations" is relatively short. The dialogue partners are aware of the hermeneutical task, but they do not elaborate on this matter. They regard Scripture as normative, and emphasize that they do not use Scripture to proof-text certain dogmatic positions.[18] What is lacking, however, is a sustained exploration of what this might mean, and how the range of terminology used might be understood.

After having described the "Following of Jesus and the Mission of the Twelve"[19] as well as the "Commission of the Risen Christ and the Promise of the Holy Spirit,"[20] Part 1 offers a thorough examination of the understanding of ἀπόστολος and ἀποστολή in the New Testament. Starting with detailed terminological observations, the document then analyzes the meaning and implications of the term ἀπόστολος in the Pauline Corpus as well as in Luke and Acts.

A particularly important point is made in paragraph 25 with its emphasis upon the role of the apostles as being both foundational and formative. An apostle's foundational role "implies a responsibility for setting a norm that may subsequently be further explored, developed, and

---

17. *Apostolicity of the Church*, introduction.

18. A detailed examination of whether the commission's selection and theological emphasis on biblical scripture is a matter of proof-texting certain dogmatic positions or not would be beyond the scope of this paper.

19. Cf. *Apostolicity of the Church*, §§5–9.

20. Cf. ibid., §§10–13.

applied, but not abandoned and distorted."[21] An apostle is described as being both an example- and tradition-bearer, and successor ministries are bound to follow in the wake of this example. This point is also stressed in Part 3 which deals with one of the thorniest of all ecumenical issues: the recognition of ministries. The "Biblical Orientation" introducing Part 3 emphasizes that succession to the apostles is not just a matter of continuity in function and office but also a matter of apostolic life.[22] The particular emphasis on the "following of Jesus Christ,"[23] the so-called "apostolicity of life," is one of the most positive examples of the reception of New Testament concepts of Apostolicity. The apostolicity of life is also acknowledged by stressing that the "*depositum fidei* also comprises a *depositum vitae*, inviting the community to imitate the apostolic life in its spiritual discipline and practices."[24]

Part 1 continues by describing "Ecclesial Structures and Patterns of Ministry"[25] reflected in the canonical writings of the New Testament. This part emphasizes that the early Church was never without leaders.[26] It stresses both the foundational role of the apostles and the Pastoral Epistles' clear evidence of a concern for faithful continuation of the essence of the apostles' work after their departure, a concern inevitably related to the commissioning of faithful successors.[27] In order to truly reflect the variety of the notions of apostle in the New Testament, it must not be overlooked that Acts does mention other apostles, not only Peter. Even the encyclical

---

21. Ibid., §25.

22. Cf. "In the New Testament, 'apostolic succession' takes place within the horizon of following Jesus Christ ... Understood on this way, 'apostolic succession' maintains the uniqueness proper to the ministry of the apostles while mediating it, within the horizon of the following of Jesus Christ, to an ongoing ministry for building up the church on the foundation of Jesus Christ which the apostles once laid" (ibid., §183). The Lutheran World Federation document *Episcopal Ministry within the Apostolicity of the Church* (2007) reinforces this with a quotation from Luther: "Now if the apostles, evangelists and prophets are no longer living, others must have replaced them and will replace them until the end of the world, for the Church shall last until the end of the world, and so apostles, evangelists and prophets must therefore remain, no matter what their name, to promote God's word and work" (ibid., §25).

23. *Apostolicity of the Church*, §183.

24. Ibid., §172.

25. Ibid., §§35–53.

26. Cf. ibid.

27. Cf. Carter, *Apostolicity of the Church—Assessment and Critique*, 2.

Ut unum sint. On commitment to Ecumenism (1995) by Pope John Paul II provides a much more ecumenical reading of this passage.[28]

The majority of the first part revisits certain conclusions of modern scholars which have become widely accepted across the confessional boundaries concerning the meaning of "apostle," the nature of ministry as emerging within New Testament times and evidenced within the biblical canon. Nevertheless, very few sections subscribe to the way special biblical quotes have been used to back doctrine, and recent scholarship is not included. One example is the support for female apostles, which is only mentioned in passing, and does not include reference to recent research on this topic.[29]

Parts 2, 3, and 4 clearly set out traditional Roman Catholic and Lutheran teachings on the topics concerned, with particular emphasis upon more modern developments, especially those that have allowed a degree of rapprochement. The authors record and interface, sometimes even emphasizing continuing differences, but then look for convergence. The method used throughout the document is that of a "differentiated consensus" in which "the remaining differences have been shown not to be church-dividing."[30] The hope is expressed that through a common acceptance of a differentiated consensus on apostolicity, reconciliation in questions (e.g., the core of the gospel, or papal activity) may come.[31]

Part 2 "The Apostolic Gospel and the Apostolicity of the Church" examines in detail the relation between the apostolic gospel and the ecclesial attribute of apostolicity. It highlights the extent to which the two communions have moved from originally opposed positions towards a common rapprochement in their understanding of the core of the Gospel. Part 2 includes a couple of sections which consider the underlying hermeneutical "Vorverständnis," which is "the preconception" or "prior understanding" of the dialogue partners. However, this part does not discuss biblical hermeneutics, only stating existing differences regarding the question of how scripture is to be interpreted with integrity. This is seen as directly

---

28. Cf. *Ut unum sint*, §§55, 90, and 97.

29. Cf. *Apostolicity of the Church*, §8. However, as it was decided at the beginning of the study that the question of ordination of women would be left out, not considering female apostles is a consequence of this primary decision.

30. Ibid., §431.

31. Cf. a sub-section of Part 2 titled "Diversity and Its Reconciliation," in ibid., §§124–43.

linked to the question about the role of the magisterium, the "teaching authority" of the Roman Catholic Church.[32] The fourth and final part of the document, entitled "Church Teaching that Remains in the Truth,"[33] takes up hermeneutical issues when describing how church teaching remains in the truth revealed in the gospel of Jesus Christ. In the final summary, hermeneutical issues regarding the Scriptures and the biblical canon are mentioned among the points of complete agreement. The dialogue partners agree that "the Scriptures are the source, rule, guideline and criterion for the correctness and purity of the Church's proclamation" and that "by the biblical canon, the Church does not constitute but recognises the authority of the prophetic and apostolic scriptures."[34]

The "Biblical Introduction" to Part 3 "Apostolic Succession and Ordained Ministry" shows that the Commission was attentive to the dynamic of development within the New Testament itself. It reflects the ambiguity of the term "apostle," particularly as used by Paul, sometimes confined to the witnesses of the resurrection, whose function is untransmittable *per se*, but also sometimes used apparently in a wider context to connote roving missionaries who had not necessarily been witnesses to the resurrection. It notes that, later, the term became confined to the Eleven and to other exceptional witnesses of the resurrection, Paul included.[35]

Part 3 stresses the significance of the transmission of the apostolic legacy and the means whereby this is accomplished through the laying on of hands and prayer in respect of those who have that particular responsibility within the Church. It must be valued positively that the ambiguity of the New Testament evidence concerning the relationship between spiritual gifts and the laying on of hands is acknowledged.[36]

CONCLUDING REFLECTIONS

Even this brief examination of *The Apostolicity of the Church* indicates that there are still major issues relating to the joint interpretation and

---

32. Cf. ibid., §§144–64.
33. Cf. ibid., §§294–460.
34. Cf. ibid., §§432–34.
35. Cf. Carter, *Apostolicity of the Church*, 2.
36. Acts 8 seems to imply that the laying on of hands is in recognition of gifts already bestowed whereas "Paul" in the Pastoral Epistles clearly sees a charism as being given in and through the laying on of hands (cf. ibid., 3).

reception of the concept of apostolicity in ecumenical documents which need to be explored more thoroughly and more openly. However, it must be acknowledged that the use of the Bible is thorough, and that the authors of this text take great care to largely avoid the danger of prooftexting certain existing dogmatic positions by painting a "biblical picture" on apostolicity based in biblical scholarship at the beginning of the document, which then forms the underpinning for the subsequent discussion of the subject. The advantage of this approach is that it establishes a biblical foundation to which subsequent discussion can return and expand, but which from the very start expresses the variety of uses of the term "apostles" in the Bible and acknowledges the issues that arise from this. This attempt is impressive and effective and sets a very high standard for the use of Biblical Scriptures in subsequent ecumenical dialogue.

However, problems which can emerge in the use of the Bible in ecumenical documents have also been noted in this paper. In order to express the true diversity of the Bible and its interpretations some examples of differing interpretations from the same biblical texts might need to be given, both from biblical scholarship and from different denominations. This may involve exploring the debates in biblical scholarship about certain disputed texts and reflecting these scholarly discussions in the body of the document. Offering different examples would acknowledge and illustrate the diversity that can exist in biblical interpretation and reception before moving towards a more common statement which reflects the unity that arises out of this diversity. This approach would require detailed biblical and hermeneutical work as the foundation for discussion. The advantage of this approach would be not only to provide a firm basis within the Bible and the potential to reflect the diversity that exists both within it and within biblical scholarship, but also fruitful insights and new departures on contested ecumenical issues.[37]

---

37. Cf. Paula Gooder, "According to the Scriptures,'" 90.

BIBLIOGRAPHY

Burkhard, John J. *Apostolicity Then and Now. An Ecumenical Church in a Postmodern World.* Collegeville, MN: Liturgical, 2004.

Carter, David. *The Apostolicity of the Church—Assessment and Critique.* Catholic Bishops' Conference of England and Wales and Lutheran Council of Great Britain, 17. June 2008 (unpublished).

Frey, Jörg. *Apostelbegriff, Apostelamt und Apostolizität: Neutestamentliche Perspektiven zur Frage nach der „Apostolizität' der Kirche.* In *Das kirchliche Amt in apostolischer Nachfolge I. Grundlagen und Grundfragen,* edited by Theodor Schneider and Gunther Wenz, 91–198. Freiburg: Herder, 2004.

Gaventa, Beverly Roberts. "Interpreting Scriptures Together: Seeking the Visible Unity of the Church." *Journal of Ecumenical Studies* 43 (2008) 309–19.

Gooder, Paula. "'According to the Scriptures . . .': The Use of the Bible in Baptism, Eucharist and Ministry." In *Paths to Unity: Explorations in Ecumenical Method,* edited by Paul Avis, 75–90. London: Church House Publishing, 2004.

Hahn, Ferdinand. "Apostel. I. Neues Testament." In *Religion in Geschichte und Gegenwart,* 4th ed., edited by Hans Dieter Betz et al., 1:636–38. Tübingen: Mohr/Siebeck, 1998.

Kertelge, Karl. "Apostel." In *Lexikon für Theologie und Kirche,* 1:851–54. Freiburg: Herder, 1993.

Meier, John P. "The Circle of the Twelve: Did It Exist during Jesus' Public Ministry?" *Journal of Biblical Literature* 116 (1997) 635–72.

Roloff, Jürgen. "Apostel/Apostolat/Apostolizität." In *Theologische Realenzyklopädie,* edited by Gerhard Krause and Gerhard Müller, 3:430–45. Berlin: de Gruyter, 1978.

Schnackenburg, Rudolf. "Apostles before and during Paul's Time." In *Apostolic History and the Gospel: Biblical and Historical Essays Presented to F. F. Bruce on His 60th Birthday,* edited by W. Ward Gasque and Ralph P. Martin, 287–303. Grand Rapids: Eerdmans, 1970.

———. "Apostolicity—The Present Position of Studies." *One in Christ* 6 (1970) 243–73.

Tetley, Joy. "The Use of the Bible in Ecumenical Dialogue involving Anglicans." In *Paths to Unity: Explorations in Ecumenical Method,* edited by Paul Avis, 52–69. London: Church House Publishing, 2004.

Wenz, Gunther. "Von Aposteln und apostolischer Nachfolge." *Una Sancta: Zeitschrift für ökumenische Bewegung* 1 (2007) 52–72.

Ecumenical Documents

"Church and Justification." In *Growth in Agreement II. Reports and Agreed Statements of Ecumenical Conversations on a World Level, 1982–1998,* edited by Jeffrey Gros, Harding Meyer, and William G. Rusch, 485–565. Geneva: WCC Publications, 2000.

"Malta Report." In *Growth in Agreement. Reports and Agreements of Ecumenical Conversations on a World Level,* edited by H. Meyer and L. Vischer, 168–89. New York: Paulist, 1984.

The Apostolicity of the Church: Study Document of the Lutheran-Roman Catholic Commission on Unity. The Lutheran World Federation & Pontifical Council for Promoting Christian Unity. Minneapolis: Lutheran University Press, 2006.

Ut unum sint: Encyclical Letter of the Holy Father John Paul II on Commitment to Ecumenism. London: Catholic Truth Society, 1995.

10

Defense and Disputation, Erudition and Exchange
An Overview of the History of New Testament Translations into Hebrew

Murray Watson

Depending upon one's perspective, the idea that the Christian Scriptures should exist in Hebrew is either something more or less self-evident and reasonable, or something that is odd, confusing, inappropriate and potentially offensive. For the 'parting of the ways' that took place between Christian Jews and their non-Christian coreligionists was not simply a rupture on a *theological* level; it was *also*, in many ways, a distancing on the levels of *geography, culture* and, very importantly, on the level of *language*. Indeed, the divergent paths taken by the Jewish and Christian communities in the centuries since have been deeply influenced by the fact that *one* group remained—and *has remained*—faithful to the Hebrew language which was the ancient heritage of *both* groups, while the *other* very quickly translated its message into the words and thought-forms of the Greek-speaking world and, not long after that, into the Latin language of the Romans. This Hebrew-versus-Greek dichotomy, which has provided such rich fodder for generations of Biblical scholars, has also marked a theological *boundary* between these two faiths, a linguistic chasm that neither Jews nor Christians were expected to cross: Hebrew and Aramaic for the Jews, Greek and Latin for the Christians—and never the twain shall meet.

Of course, the lines were never quite as neatly drawn as that image might suggest. The majority of Jews, even in Jesus's time, lived in the

Diaspora, using Greek as their daily language, and, for many, reading or hearing the Scriptures of Israel in their Greek versions. Christian communities, furthermore, have continued to live in the land of Israel and its neighbors for the 2,000 years since, some of whom preserved their faith in Hebrew's sister-languages of Aramaic and Syriac, which are still used liturgically in several Eastern-rite Catholic and Orthodox churches to this day. But, generally speaking, Hebrew was *lingua non grata* for Christians, and the Greek New Testament was beyond the pale for Jews. It was *theological positions* which increasingly and sometimes *violently* opposed the two faiths—Christians seeing the Jews as 'blinded', rejected by God, refusing to acknowledge the truth of the Messiah's coming and, in extreme cases, as agents of the Devil. Jews, on the other hand, tended to define Christians as a dangerous group of apostates, whose interpretation of the Bible was mistaken, whose Messiah was either a failure or a fraud, and who had broken ranks with God's covenant people by Trinitarian innovations which made a mockery of the divine unity proclaimed in the *Shema Yisrael*. The theology was the *substance* of the divide, but the languages were effectively its *symbol* and *medium*.

It therefore comes as a surprise to many of us to discover that, beyond the antagonistic rhetoric that separated the two communities, there has almost never been a time in which at least *portions* of the Christian Scriptures have not existed in Hebrew translations, however fragmentary. For many Christians, this is wholly understandable; after all, as the Third Quest for the historical Jesus has hammered home, Jesus of Nazareth *was*, and *remained*, a Palestinian Jew from his birth to his death. His prayers and worship were predominantly in Hebrew and, depending on which scholars you side with, his daily language would either have been Aramaic, with an occasional use of Hebrew, or Hebrew, with an occasional use of Aramaic.[1] He lived and died in a Semitic world, spoke Semitic languages,

---

1. Leaning more toward Hebrew: M. H. Segal, "Mishnaic Hebrew and its Relation to Biblical Hebrew and to Aramaic," *Jewish Quarterly Review* 20 (1908) 670–700; Segal, *Grammar of Mishnaic Hebrew* (Oxford: Clarendon, 1927) 5–19; H. Birkeland, *The Language of Jesus* (Oslo: Dybwad, 1954); Chaim Rabin ("Hebrew and Aramaic in the First Century," in *The Jewish People in the First Century*, ed. S. Safrai and M. Stern, vol. 2 [Philadelphia: Fortress, 1976], 1007–39); Shmuel Safrai, "Spoken Languages in the Time of Jesus," n.p., online: www.jerusalemperspective.com; leaning more toward Aramaic: Joseph A. Fitzmyer, "The Languages of Palestine in the First Century A.D." in *The Semitic Background of the New Testament. Part 2: A Wandering Aramean* (Grand Rapids: Eerdmans, 1997), 29–56; Bruce Chilton and Craig A. Evans, *Studying the Historical Jesus:*

and prayed as part of the assembly of Israel. Though this fact has been obscured by centuries of Greek, Latin and other vernacular translations, Christians are today recovering this insight with enthusiasm and curiosity. Indeed, 'Jesus the Jew' has become so axiomatic in scholarly literature in the last thirty years that it is hard to imagine Christians ever believing otherwise.[2]

While some continue to argue for original (and now lost) Hebrew or Aramaic versions of various New Testament books, the fact remains that the earliest fragments of the New Testament that we possess in Hebrew seem to be found in rabbinic literature. The Israeli scholar and rabbi Pinchas Lapide, whose work *Hebrew in the Church: The Foundations of Jewish Christian Dialogue*[3] is one of the key studies of this question, identifies three passages which seem to be alluding to the New Testament, although in somewhat garbled form.[4] He points to a line in tractate *Šabbat*

Evaluations of the State of Current Research, NTTS 19 (Leiden: Brill, 1994) 127–28 (and many others). James Barr seems to suggest that he has adjusted his own views on this question, and has recently arrived at a somewhat more middle-of-the-road view: "when we consider the language situation of (say) the first century C.E., it can no longer be assumed that the emphasis must lie on Aramaic to the exclusion of Hebrew. On the question, in what language the teaching of Jesus was given, an increasing number of scholars in recent years has considered Hebrew as a responsible hypothesis, although the evidence for Aramaic continues to be rather stronger ... The Qumran evidence ... convinced many that Hebrew was still alive and in use as a spoken medium." ("Hebrew, Aramaic and Greek in the Hellenistic Age," in *The Cambridge History of Judaism*, ed. W. D. Davies et al. (Cambridge: Cambridge University Press, 2006) 83.

On this, see in particular the excellent bibliography in Stanley E. Porter, "The Criterion of Greek Language and Its Context," in *The Criteria for Authenticity in Historical-Jesus Research: Previous Discussion and New Proposals*, JSNTSup 191 (Sheffield: Sheffield Academic, 2000) 131–32.

2. On this, see in particular: John P. Meier, "The Present State of the 'Third Quest' for the Historical Jesus: Loss and Gain," in *Bib* 80 (1999) 459–87 (NB his conclusion on p. 486, about the theological necessity of affirming Jesus's Jewishness as a consequence of the Chalcedonian definition of the Incarnation); and Amy-Jill Levine, *The Misunderstood Jew: The Church and the Scandal of the Jewish Jesus* (San Francisco: HarperSanFrancisco, 2006), as well as many of the relevant works of David Flusser, Geza Vermes, James H. Charlesworth, et al.

3. Grand Rapids: Eerdmans, 1984; trans. of *Hebräisch in den Kirchen: Forschungen zum jüdisch-christlichen Dialoge* (Neukirchen-Vluyn: Neukirchener, 1976).

4. Lapide, *Hebrew in the Church*, 22–23. On these and related issues, see also Peter Schäfer's excellent recent book, *Jesus in the Talmud* (Princeton: Princeton University Press, 2007).

of the Babylonian Talmud (folio 116a)[5] which certainly seems a very close rendering of Matt 5:17.[6] The fact that it occurs in a context that appears, shortly afterward, to speak of the Christian writings as "the iniquity of the scroll" [עוון גליון] tends to corroborate Lapide's claim.[7] Similarly, a fragment of a polemical text recovered from the Cairo Geniza, perhaps from the middle of the ninth century, seems to contain an allusion to Jesus's crucifixion, from Matt 24:34: "They gave him lime (?) in vinegar to drink, and God will not save him . . . in the presence of those who persecute him." An Aramaic translation of the names of the Trinity shortly afterward, and mentions of specifically Christian theological terminology, make this identification highly plausible. Finally, a line in the *Duties of the Heart* (an eleventh-century Arabic Jewish work by the Spanish rabbi and philosopher Bachya ibn Paquda later translated into Hebrew) contains a loose rendering of Matt 5:33–37.[8] Admittedly, these are very few texts, covering a period of more than 500 years, but they do seem to demonstrate knowledge of *some* parts of the Gospel by prominent Hebrew-speaking Jewish leaders, in contexts which seem to imply both a defense against Christianity, and a deprecation of some key Christian claims. It seems likely that any early Hebrew renderings of the Christian Scriptures would have been for *defensive* purposes, to inoculate Jewish communities against Christian proselytizing, and perhaps to disparage Christian missionaries. The limited evidence makes it dangerous to extrapolate—but it *does* provide intriguing evidence of at least *some* permeation of the divide

---

5. "I have not come to detract from the Law of Moses, nor have I come to add to the Law of Moses."

6. "Do not think that I have come to abolish the law or the prophets; I have come not to abolish but to fulfil." NRSV.

7. "This is a scornful play on the Greek word for the gospel, *evangelion*. *Avon* means sin in Hebrew, so that *avon gilyon* would be the scripture of the sinners, or a scripture which represents the way of a sin." Yaakov Y. Teppler, *Birkat HaMinim: Jews and Christians in Conflict in the Ancient World* (Tübingen: Mohr/Siebeck, 2007) 128.

8. "And one of the pious said to his disciples:'The Law permits us to swear to the truth in the name of the Creator. But I tell you not to swear by Him, whether truly or falsely. Say yes or no.'" Cf. Matt 5:33–37: "Again, you have heard that it was said to those of ancient times, 'You shall not swear falsely, but carry out the vows you have made to the Lord'. But I say to you, Do not swear at all, either by heaven, for it is the throne of God, or by the earth, for it is his footstool, or by Jerusalem, for it is the city of the great King. And do not swear by your head, for you cannot make one hair white or black. Let your word be 'Yes, Yes' or 'No, No'; anything more than this comes from the evil one." NRSV.

on the Jewish side, even if it was only to arm oneself against the depredations of Christian preaching.

The next category of Hebrew renderings comes from the *Christian* side, and consists of limited—and often faulty—translations of New Testament texts into Hebrew, preserved only as transliterations in Roman letters. Beginning during the Carolingian Renaissance, in the mid-ninth century, a number of versions of the Lord's Prayer survive which are clearly retroversions of this key text into some form of Mishnaic Hebrew. In the second chapter of his book, Lapide provides a helpful overview of these texts, but the single most thorough investigation is provided by Father Jean Carmignac (†1986), a French pioneer in study of the Dead Sea Scrolls, and a distinguished scholar of Biblical and Qumran Hebrew. Carmignac spent his final years tracking down, researching and publishing Hebrew versions of the New Testament,[9] including critical printed editions of four of the most noteworthy.[10] In a 1978 essay, Carmignac provided an annotated inventory of almost seventy Hebrew translations of the Lord's Prayer,[11] beginning with some of these early mediæval texts, which seem to be back-translations from the Vulgate. The first, found today in the State Library in Düsseldorf, is written in a late-ninth-century missal, and contains the Hebrew text in Roman letters. A second version, dated to the ninth or tenth centuries, is found in a manuscript bequeathed to a hospital in the town of Bernkastel-Cues by Cardinal Nicholas of Cusa (†1464). Several similar texts can be found in the Bodleian Library at Oxford, dating from the twelfth through fifteenth centuries. Were they used for personal devotional purposes by individual monks who were curious about Hebrew and studied it covertly? Do they represent contact with nearby Jewish communities, and with rabbis who perhaps were willing to teach Christian students (or who did so under duress)? Or might they bear testimony to Jewish converts to Christianity—many of whom joined religious orders in this period—who were perhaps nostalgic for Hebrew, and who translated Latin prayers back into Hebrew, so as not to forget it entirely—or for the benefit of their confrères? For the time be-

---

9. See particularly Carmignac's *La naissance des Évangiles synoptiques* (Paris: O.E.I.L., 1984), and especially his second chapter, "Traductions antérieures." (English translation: *The Birth of the Synoptic Gospels* [Chicago: Franciscan Herald, 1987]).

10. Carmignac, *Traductions hébraïques des Évangiles, rassemblées par Jean Carmignac*.

11. Carmignac, "Hebrew Translations of the Lord's Prayer: An Historical Survey."

ing, such questions are not answerable on the basis of our evidence—but these texts remain an enticing mystery from a period when Hebrew was assumed to have been expunged from Christianity, and before tools for the study of Hebrew were readily available in Europe.

Some of the most extensive pre-printing Hebrew translations come from the Middle Ages, when Christianity was more aggressively targeting the Jews for conversion. One of the more favored methods was the *public disputation,* in which Christian theologians and local Jewish scholars would debate publicly for the entertainment of crowds at festival times. Although the disputations were largely staged attempts by Christian societies to demonstrate the falsity and inferiority of Judaism, they seem to have spurred a number of rabbis to prepare Hebrew editions of large sections of the New Testament, precisely to enable Jewish speakers to address Christian interlocutors knowledgeably on the basis of the Christians' *own* sacred texts. The *Book of Nestor Ha-Komer,* likely dated toward the tenth century, incorporates more than 25 quotations from the New Testament on theologically contentious topics. A number of scholars have suggested that the 'Nestor' referred to may, in fact, be the fifth-century Eastern bishop Nestorius (†451), whose views, condemned at the Council of Ephesus in 431, were popularly caricatured by his opponents as "Jewish" or "judaizing," because of their apparent denial of the reality of the Incarnation.[12] Daniel Lasker[13] argues convincingly that this Hebrew text is based on an earlier *Arabic* text, *Qiṣṣat Mujādalat al-Usquf* [The Account of the Disputation of the Bishop],[14] probably dating back

---

12. "When news of Nestorius' deposition reached Constantinople, the *Coptic Acts of Ephesus* report that crowds expressed their joy by shouting, 'Nestorius the Jew!' Four days later, another anti-Nestorian crowd gathered in the Great Church chanting, 'Nestorius and the thirty men are Jews.'" (Susan Wessel, *Cyril of Alexandria and the Nestorian Controversy: The Making of a Saint and of a Heretic,* Oxford Early Christian Studies [Oxford: Oxford University Press, 2004], 217).

"It was common to castigate opponents of Nicene orthodoxy as Judaizers, on the grounds that, as Subordinationists, they recognized God the Father, but failed to pay proper honour to God the Son." (in Evagrius Scholasticus, *The Ecclesiastical History of Evagrius Scholasticus,* trans. Michael Whitby, Translated Texts for Historians 33 [Liverpool: Liverpool University Press, 2000] 7 n11).

13. "*Qiṣṣat Mujādalat al-Usquf* and *Nestor Ha-Komer:* The Earliest Arabic and Hebrew Anti-Christian Polemics," in *Geniza Research After Ninety Years: The Case of Judæo-Arabic,* ed. Joshua Blau and Stefan C. Reif (New York: Cambridge University Press, 1992) 112–18.

14. [Ed.—Transliterations of Hebrew and Aramaic follow the originals cited.]

to the ninth century, and which appears to be the earliest extended Jewish polemic against Christianity. Nestor was, of course, followed by *other* similar treatises, including the mid-twelfth-century *Sefer Milḥamot ha-Shem* [the *Book of the Wars of the Lord*] by Jacob ben Reuben (†ca. 1200),[15] whose eleventh chapter contains nineteen lengthy quotations from the Gospel of Matthew. In 1274, the French rabbi Joseph Official published his *Sefer Yoseph ha-Meqanne'* [the *Book of Joseph the Zealous*], containing 40 substantial New Testament texts in Hebrew translation or paraphrase.[16] Although these, and a number of other polemical works, argue vehemently *against* Christianity, relations between European rabbis and Christian clergy were not always so polemical, and there seems at time to have been friendly discussions between leaders of the two communities. Many of the distinguished Jewish thinkers of this period, including Saadia Gaon, Judah ha-Levi and Maimonides, demonstrate a sometimes surprising degree of familiarity with the New Testament and Christian interpretation.

One of the more vexed questions in this field relates to the existence of several mediæval manuscripts of the Gospel of Matthew entirely in Hebrew.[17] In the late fourteenth century, the Jewish polemicist Shemtob ibn Shaprut incorporated a Hebrew translation of Matthew in his work *'Eben*

---

15. See Lapide, *Hebrew in the Church*, 25–30. The original title of the work was *Sepher ha-Mekaḥed weha-Meyaḥed* [The Book of the Denier and the Affirmer].

16. "The Paris manuscript of the book presents an extensive criticism of the New Testament in its last eight pages. It contains forty Hebrew quotations from the New Testament, of one to eight verses each, and eleven quotations from the Latin Vulgate in Hebrew transliteration . . . While quotations from Matthew represent the majority (twenty-five in all) and are generally the best translated, five of the remaining fifteen quotations are merely paraphrases of New Testament passages . . . Only two passages in Matthew (8:1–4; 28:16–19) are cited by both the *Sefer Milḥamot ha-Shem* of Jakob ben Reuben and the Paris manuscript of Joseph the Zealous, but the differences between them make it quite clear that the latter had no knowledge of the earlier." (Lapide, *Hebrew in the Church*, 31)

17. The material below on Hebrew translations of Matthew is largely drawn from George Howard's *Hebrew Gospel of Matthew* (Macon, GA: Mercer University Press, 1995); Howard is one of the main contemporary scholars of these manuscripts, and this book represents a second revised (and more nuanced) version of his earlier *The Gospel of Matthew According to a Primitive Hebrew Text* (Macon, GA: Mercer University Press, 1987). See also William Horbury, "The Hebrew Text of Matthew in Shem Tob ibn Shaprut's *Eben Boḥan*" in W. D. Davies and Dale C. Allison, *A Critical and Exegetical Commentary on the Gospel According to Saint Matthew*, 3 vols., ICC (London: Continuum, 1997) 3:729–38.

Boḥan [The Touchstone]. The apparent similarity of some of its wordings with earlier Jewish quotations of Matthew in Hebrew has led some to speculate that it might be rooted in a much earlier Hebrew Matthew (which some associate with the Hebrew gospel of Matthew referred to by several Church Fathers). Whether ibn Shaprut was himself the composer of this text, or whether he inherited it from an earlier tradition, remains debated: Matthew Black seems to believe that ibn Shaprut *was* its author,[18] while William Horbury concludes otherwise.[19]

In 1537, Sebastian Münster (†1552)—a noted cartographer, mathematician and Franciscan monk-turned-Lutheran exegete—published at Basel a Hebrew edition of Matthew, entitled *The Torah of the Messiah* [תורת המשיח],[20] based upon a manuscript that he claimed to have received in defective form from the Jewish community. Unfortunately, Münster does not distinguish between this document's original readings and his own editorial reconstructions, and the manuscript from which he worked is no longer extant.

In 1555, a somewhat *different* Hebrew Matthew was published in Paris by Jean Mercier, together with his own Latin translation. The edition, entitled *Besorat Mattai* [The Good News of Matthew], was based on a manuscript that he had received from his friend Jean du Tillet, the bishop of Saint-Brieuc.[21] The circumstances of its provenance are somewhat dubious: Du Tillet said that he had "discovered" the manuscript during a journey to Italy in 1553, but several scholars have pointed out that it was precisely at this time that the Pope had decreed the confiscation of all Hebrew books from Rome's Jewish community.[22] It seems likely that

---

18. "The author of the Hebrew Matthew was probably a certain Shem-Tob ben Shaprut, a famous Jewish polemical writer who flourished in Spain in the fourteenth century." *An Aramaic Approach to the Gospels and Acts*, 3rd ed. (Peabody, MA: Hendrickson, 1998) 295.

19. "Ibn Shaprut himself does not present himself as a translator in his treatment of the gospels, and is most unlikely to have made a translation of Matthew entirely anew," in Davies and Allison, *Critical and Exegetical Commentary*, 3:730).

20. The New York Public Library's research collection of rare Judaica holds a 1557 edition of this work titled *Evangelium secundum Matthæum in lingua hebraica, cum versione latina, atque annotationibus Seb. Munsteri ; unà cum Epistola D. Pauli ad Hebræos, hebraicè & latinè*.

21. According to Lapide, this manuscript is today preserved at the Bibliothèque Nationale in Paris, as Hebrew Ms. 132.

22. See, for example, Amnon Raz-Krakotzkin, "Censorship, Editing, and the Reshaping of Jewish Identity: The Catholic Church and Hebrew Literature in the Sixeenth Century,"

Du Tillet's Hebrew Matthew was one of those books, and obtained under conditions that were less than morally impeccable. Although it seems likely that these two versions are variously derived from some common ancestor, the exact nature of their relationship and evolution remains the subject of debate.[23]

In the wake of the Protestant Reformation, the renewed emphasis on the centrality of the Bible sparked a renaissance of Hebrew study and translation, and a number of scholars produced translations of portions of the New Testament, most notably the Gospels that were used in the liturgical lectionary.[24] The first translation of the entire New Testament in Hebrew, however, had to wait until 1599. The German Protestant theologian and Biblical scholar Elias Hutter (†ca. 1609) had determined to issue his own ground-breaking polyglot edition of the Bible, in no less than twelve languages: Greek, Latin, Syriac, German, Bohemian, Italian, Spanish, French, English, Danish, Polish, . . . and Hebrew. Since Hutter had been unable to locate a Hebrew version of the entire New Testament, he undertook to produce his own translation. Hutter's version,[25] which

---

in *Hebraica Veritas? Christian Hebraists and the Study of Judaism in Early Modern Europe*, ed. Allison Coudert and Jeffrey S. Shoulson, Jewish Culture and Contexts (Philadelphia: University of Pennsylvania Press, 2004): "In September 1553, by a decree of the Roman Inquisition, all copies of the Talmud that were found in Rome were gathered, and on the ninth of that month (Rosh Hashanah), they were set on fire in the Campo dei Fiori, the square that during the sixteenth and seventeenth centuries witnessed many burnings, both of books and of human beings. On the twelfth of September, a bull signed by Pope Julius III was sent throughout the Catholic world, demanding the confiscation and burning of all copies of the Talmud. The detailed decree explained that the Talmud provides clear evidence that the Jews have abandoned the Bible of Moses, and that it contains passages contrary to the laws of morality and nature, along with blasphemous vituperations against Christianity" (125).

23. In 1879, Adolf Herbst reprinted the two texts, in an early attempt at a critical edition, assuming both of them to be variants of the earlier Shemtob version. See: A. Herbst, *Des Schemtob ben Schaphrut hebraeische Übersetzung des Evangeliums Matthaei nach den Drucken des S. Münster und J. du Tillet-Mercier neu herausgegeben* (Göttingen: Dieterich, 1879). See also: William Horbury, "The Hebrew Matthew and Hebrew Study," in *Hebrew Study from Ezra to ben-Yehuda*, ed. William Horbury (Edinburgh: T. & T. Clark, 1999) 122–34.

24. Fredericus Petri issued his *Evangelia Anniversaria: quae Dominicis diebus et sanctorum festis leguntur, Hebraice conversa*, beginning in 1573, and subsequently reprinted and re-edited by others.

25. *Novum Testamentum Dnī: Nrī: Iesu. Christi. Syriacè, Italicè, Ebraicè, Hispanicè, Græcè, Gallicè, Latinè, Anglicè, Germanicè, Danicè, Bohemicè, Polonicè. Studio et Laborè Eliæ Hutteri, Germani. Norimbergæ. Cumgratia et privilegio Sac: Cæs: Mtis: ad quindecim annos*. M.D.CXIX.

came to be known as the "Nuremberg Polyglot," represents the pinnacle of the Renaissance printer's art, requiring the hand-setting of fonts of type for at least six different alphabets. It is also of interest to students of the Hebrew language, since Hutter introduced the innovation of printing the three Hebrew radicals of each word in *solid* letters, while letters added for morphological reasons were printed in *hollow* letters; root-letters which were assimilated or omitted were indicated by tiny superscript letters at the appropriate location. Hutter's edition, somewhat revised, was reprinted in 1661 by William Robertson in London,[26] and this, in turn, was re-edited in a slightly corrected version by the Englishman William Caddick in 1798.[27] In this way, Hutter's influence continued to be felt well

---

In his history of Hebrew translations, however, Jean Carmignac states that an earlier translation of the New Testament into Hebrew had been prepared around 1360 by the Byzantine monk and humanist Simon Atoumanos (later archbishop of Thebes), but that the manuscript was lost two centuries later in the library of Genoa. (*La Naissance des Évangiles synoptiques.* Paris: O.E.I.L, 1984, p. 16). Unfortunately, he provides no source for this assertion. James Townley (*Illustrations of Biblical Literature, Exhibiting the History and Fate of the Sacred Writings, from the Earliest Period to the Present Century . . .* Vol. 2. New York: Carlton and Porter, 1856, p. 351) quotes Paulus Freherus (*Theatrum virorum eruditione clarorum.* Nuremberg, 1688, vol. 2, Part 4, p. 1474) as saying that the true pioneer in this field was a *different* German, Erasmus Oswaldus Schreccefuchsius [Schreckenfuchsius] (1511–1579), a student of Sebastian Münster in languages, mathematics and cartography. This claim would seem to be buttressed by Melchior Adam's *Vitæ Germanorum philosophorum, qui seculo superiori, et quod excurrit, philosophicis ac humanioribus literis clari floruerunt* (Heidelberg: Typis Johannis Lacelloti, 1615): "Inter alias quoque lucubrationes *Testamentum Novum* in Hebraicam linguam primus transtulit" (p. 300). Adam notes that it was Schreckenfuchsius who delivered the funeral oration for Münster—in Hebrew. See the scanned version of Adam's entry for Schreckenfuchsius, available online, beginning at: http://www.uni-mannheim.de/mateo/camenaref/adam/adam1/s315.html.

26. *Novum Testamentum Hebraicum, emendatum et Castigatum opera et studio Guliel Robertsonii* (London: Roycroft Press, 1661).

27. *The New Testament of Our Lord and Saviour Jesus Christ, in Hebrew; corrected from the version published by Dr. Hutter, at Nuremburg, 1599; and republished by Dr. Robertson, at London, 1661* (London: T. Plummer, 1798). Darlow and Moule's *Historical Catalogue of the Printed Editions of Holy Scripture in the Library of the British and Foreign Bible Society* states that Caddick's 1798 edition was incomplete, and included only Matthew and Mark. The *Oxford Dictionary of National Biography* entry on Caddick states that he went on to produce a three-volume Hebrew edition of the entire New Testament in 1799–1800. (Henry Bradly, "Caddick, Richard." Rev. by Philip Carter. London: Oxford University Press, 2004; online at: www.oxforddnb.com). The British Library edition is from 1805, and portions of it are printed in Hebrew, Greek, Latin, and English.

into the early nineteenth century. Later scholars praised Hutter's overall sound instincts in rendering words and concepts in Hebrew.[28]

Carmignac's *Naissance des Évangiles synoptiques* provides (pp. 15–23) an extremely thorough and fascinating overview of various other partial New Testament translations into Hebrew, including a version of the Gospels made by a small-town English curate, Thomas Lydiat (†1646), apparently as a pleasant scholarly pastime, and another made by Giovanni Battista Giona (†1668), a former rabbi born in the Holy Land, who converted to Catholicism in 1625. Giona went on to become a noted Hebrew scholar in Rome, and his 1668 translation of the Gospels[29] included a preface by Pope Clement IX. Carmignac also mentions the intriguing Hebrew translation of the New Testament which was 'discovered' by the Reverend Claudius Buchanan in the early 1800s in Cochin, south India, where it had apparently been translated by a rabbi of the 'Black Jews of Cochin' to defend against Christian missionaries.[30] That unusual manuscript was donated to Cambridge University by Buchanan, and is still part of their collection. Its exact genesis—and even the true identity of its translator—remain unclear.[31]

---

28. Franz Delitzsch, for example, wrote: "His Hebrew translation reveals a grasp of the language rare among Christians, and it is still worth consulting, for in instance after instance he has been most fortunate in striking on precisely the right expression." (*Uebersetzungsarbeit*, 27–28, as cited and translated in Lapide, *Hebrew in the Church*, 66)

29. *Quattuor Evangelia Novi Testamenti ex Latino in Hebraicum sermoneum versa* (Rome: Propaganda Fide). The Hebrew title which Giona gave to his translation was אבני הגליונים, *'bny hglywnym*, "the revealed stones," a reference to the stone tablets of the Mosaic Law, which he argued were "revealed" or "made manifest" (*petra manifestata*) in the covenant announced by Jesus.

30. H. Rabinowicz, "Cambridge University Library," in *Jewish Quarterly Review* New Series 53.1 (1962), 73. The *Oxford Dictionary of National Biography* entry on Buchanan gives a somewhat less altruistic portrayal of his manuscript-hunting expeditions: "Buchanan alienated the Jews in Cochin by taking valuable manuscripts by force, and although accounts of his travels were published in literary and religious periodicals, his zeal occasionally overran his discretion." (Penelope Carson, "Buchanan, Claudius [1766–1815]," in *Oxford Dictionary of National Biography*. Oxford: Oxford University Press, 2004; online at: www.oxforddnb.com). See also: "Notes on Hebrew MSS. in the University Library at Cambridge. VI," *Jewish Quarterly Review* 6 (1893) 144–45.

31. Gustav Dalman ("Hebrew Translations of the New Testament," in *The New Schaff-Herzog Encyclopedia of Religious Knowledge* [New York: Funk and Wagnalls, 1908] 1:148) mentions a version made by Ezekiel Rachbi (d. 1772) and an assistant from Germany, and it seems almost certain that this is the same translator mentioned by Carmignac (p. 19) as Ezekiel Raḥibi and by Lapide as Ezekiel Raḥabi, who is said to have translated almost the entire New Testament into Hebrew around 1760, a process which led to his later

The revival of missionary fervor in the early nineteenth century also led to the founding of bodies whose explicit aim was the conversion of Jews to Christianity. Among these, the best known was certainly the London Society for the Promotion of Christianity Among the Jews.[32] The most widely-read version produced in this period was the הברית החדשה of Franz Delitzsch (†1890). Delitzsch, one of the best Christian Hebraists of the nineteenth century, was dissatisfied with the then-available Hebrew versions, and undertook to produce an improved version, which would be better-suited to the sensitivities of Jews steeped in Biblical Hebrew. The first edition was published by the British and Foreign Bible Society in 1877, and it would go through eleven editions in the thirteen years before Delitzsch's death. Subsequently revised by Gustaf Dalman, the Delitzsch New Testament remains a monumental work, a standard edition still used today by many Messianic Jews and some Christians in Israel.

A separate and somewhat competing version was that prepared by Isaac Salkinson (†1883) who, upon his conversion from Judaism to Christianity, embarked on a career as a missionary to the Jews. Salkinson, who as a young man had translated both Milton and Shakespeare into Hebrew, embarked on the task of New Testament translation under the auspices of London's Trinitarian Bible Society. His almost complete translation was finished and revised after his death, by another Jewish convert, Christian David Ginsburg, and was published in 1885, followed by fifteen reprints throughout Europe and the United States. Although many readers of Hebrew have their own preference, either for Delitzsch or for Salkinson-Ginsburg, the fact is (as Delitzsch himself acknowledged) that

---

conversion. Solomon Schechter discussed these unusual texts (Oo 1:32 and 16) in the above-cited 1893 *JQR* article; he was skeptical of some of Buchanan's claims, and dismissive of the overall quality of the manuscripts concerned: "The name of the translator is not given, but Buchanan, in his *Christian Researches* (p. 316), tells us that he was a learned Rabbi 'who conceived the design of making an accurate version of the New Testament for the expression purpose of confuting it'... The story seems rather doubtful; but whatever the case may have been, we can only say that the translator performed his task very badly, his version being most inaccurate, and his Hebrew style and even spelling betraying an ignorance of the holy language unusual even with the Malabar Rabbi." However, one of the accompanying texts, a chronicle of the Malabar Jewish community, seems to put the lie to these claims:

אבל זה יחזקאל אינו רבי ומשפחתו רחבי

"This Ezekiel, however, is not a rabbi, nor is his family Raḥabi" (Schechter, 143).

32. Founded in 1809, and often referred to simply as the "London Jews' Society," today it is known as the Church's Ministry Among Jewish People [CMJ]; http://www.cmj.org.uk.

both editions borrowed ideas from each other, and are thus a result of a fruitful cross-pollination that has produced the two most widely-known and -used Hebrew New Testaments in circulation today.

The most recent attempt to render the New Testament into (modern) Hebrew is that undertaken under the auspices of the United Bible Societies (UBS). Beginning with a gathering of Protestant representatives in Israel in 1969, the decision was made to embark on a new translation of the entire New Testament. The principles of the translation were honed in the early 1970s, by means of translations of several Pauline letters. In 1976, this new version was published by the UBS, having been prepared by an interdenominational team of translators including Robert Lindsey (Baptist), Magne Solheim (Lutheran), and Gabriel Grossman, OP (Roman Catholic).[33] A further revision was issued in 1991 by the Bible Society in Israel (the local affiliate of the worldwide UBS), for which the BSI was awarded a prestigious literary prize by the Israeli government in 1993.[34] This has now become the standard edition in modern Hebrew, and has been adopted by Hebrew-speaking Catholics for use in their liturgical lectionary.[35]

Sadly, time and space do not allow here for a discussion of the related—and provocative—question of 'Hebraized' New Testaments. Suffice it to say that, since the middle of the twentieth century, a number of translations have been prepared—some by Messianic Jews, Hebrew Christians, or Christian Zionists—attempting to inject some of the lost Hebrew character back into the New Testament.[36] Some of these have been done with

---

33. Lapide, *Hebrew in the Church*, 226 n. 174. Yochanan Elihai and Joshua Blum, two Jewish converts to Catholicism, both served as consultants on the translating team (Father David Neuhaus, SJ, one of the chaplains to the Hebrew-speaking Catholic community in Israel; personal e-mail; 10 March 2008).

34. http://www.biblesocietyinisrael.com/who.htm.

35. Neuhaus, email, 10 March 2008. He notes that many Protestant and Messianic Jewish groups in Israel still prefer the Delitzsch version, which retains a more Biblical-rabbinic flavour.

36. Among these, I would include: André Chouraqui's New Testament translation (his "Jewish" version of the Gospels, *Évangiles: Les Quatre Annonces,* was first published in 1976 by Desclée de Brouwer, Paris, and later incorporated in *Un pacte neuf* [Brépols: Lidis, 1984] and in *La Bible Chouraqui* [Paris: Desclée de Brouwer, 2003 and subsequently]); David H. Stern's *Jewish New Testament: A Translation of the New Testament That Expresses Its Jewishness* (Jerusalem/Clarksville, MD: Jewish New Testament Publications, 1989 and subsequently) and its companion volume *The Jewish New Testament Commentary* (Clarksville, MD: Jewish New Testament Publications, 1992 and subsequently); Philip

the explicit purpose of making these Christian writings more palatable to Jewish readers, whereas others seek simply to bring home to Christians the profoundly *Jewish* character of Jesus and the New Testament. While their motives may at times be suspect, there is no question that they are, in fact, continuing a translational dialectic which has been taking place, in fits and spurts, almost since Christianity's earliest centuries. Perhaps a new generation—and new translations—will help Christians to rid themselves, once and for all, of the lingering effects of the Marcionite heresy, which sought to artificially sever Christianity from its Jewish and Hebrew pedigree. Perhaps these translations—far from promoting the absorption of Judaism into Christianity—will provide a basis upon which Jews and Christians can come together, in respect and mutual curiosity, to discover where, indeed, they *differ* . . . but also, for the sake of *tikkun olam*—the healing of the world—how much they truly *share*.

E. Goble's *Orthodox Jewish Brit Chadasha* (AFI International, 1997; see: http://www.afii.org/); James Scott Trimm's *Hebraic Roots Version New Testament* (Hurst, TX: Society for the Advancement of Nazarene Judaism, 2001); Wallis Barnstone's *The New Covenant, Commonly Called the New Testament: Newly Translated from the Greek and Informed by Semitic Sources* (New York: Riverhead, 2002); . . . as well as much of the work of Robert Lindsey and his colleagues (David Bivin, Roy Blizzard, David Flusser, Brad Young, etc.) in the Jerusalem School of Synoptic Research. *I wish to clearly state that my inclusion of these publications in no way constitutes my approval of them or their contents.* James Trimm's "ministry," in particular, has been beset by serious ethical and legal questions, as well as charges of financial irregularities. I include them simply to indicate a current of thought among some scholars, and some putatively Christian groups.

BIBLIOGRAPHY

Carmignac, Jean, editor. *Traductions hébraiques des Évangiles.* 5 vols. Turnhout, Belgium: Brépols, 1984. Vol. 1, *The Four Gospels / translated into Hebrew by William Greenfield in 1831*; vols. 2 & 3, *Évangiles de Matthieu et de Marc [de Luc et de Jean] / traduits en hébreu en 1668 par Giovanni Battista Iona ; retouchés en 1805 par Thomas Yeates* ; vol. 4, *Die vier Evangelien / ins Hebräische übersetzt von Franz Delitzsch (1877–1890–1902); kritischer Apparat der zwölf Auflagen von Hubert Klein*; vol. 5, *The Four Gospels / translated into Hebrew by the London Society for Promoting Christianity amongst the Jews (1838 + 1864).*

Carmignac, Jean. *La naissance des Évangiles synoptiques.* Paris: O.E.I.L., 1984. [In English: *The Birth of the Synoptic Gospels.* Translated by Michael J. Wrenn. Chicago: Franciscan Herald, 1987]

Clarke, Adam, and Edward Harwood. *A Bibliographical Dictionary Containing a Chronological Account, Alphabetically Arranged, of the Most Curious, Scarce, Useful, and Important Books, in All Departments of Literature, Which Have Been Published in Latin, Greek, Coptic, Hebrew, Samaritan, Syriac, Chaldee, Aethiopic, Arabic, Persian, Armenian, &C. from the Infancy of Printing to the Beginning of the Nineteenth Century.* London: Printed by J. Nuttall, for W. Baynes, 1802–1804. See "Hebrew Versions," VI:217–22.

Dalman, Gustaf. "Hebrew Translations of the New Testament." In *The New Schaff-Herzog Encyclopedia of Religious Knowledge Embracing Biblical, Historical, Doctrinal, and Practical Theology, and Biblical, Theological, and Ecclesiastical Biography from the Earliest Times to the Present Day*, edited by J. Jackson, Samuel Macauley, and Lefferts Augustine Loetscher, 2:148. Grand Rapids: Baker, 1966.

Darlow, T. H., and H. F. Moule, editors. *Historical Catalogue of the Printed Editions of Holy Scripture in the Library of the British and Foreign Bible Society.* 2 vols. in 4 parts. London: Bible House, 1903–1911. (Revised and expanded version published in 1968)

Dunlop, John. *Memories of Gospel Triumphs Among the Jews during the Victorian Era.* London: Partridge, 1894.

Gidney, W. T. *The History of the London Society for Promoting Christianity amongst the Jews From 1809 to 1908.* London: London Society for Promoting Christianity Amongst the Jews, 1908.

Horne, Thomas Hartwell. *An Introduction to the Critical Study and Knowledge of the Holy Scriptures.* 13th ed. London: Longmans, Greene, 1872.

Lapide, Pinchas. *Hebrew in the Church: The Foundations of Jewish-Christian Dialogue.* Translated by Erroll F. Rhodes. Grand Rapids: Eerdmans, 1984 [Translation of: *Hebräisch in den Kirchen: Forschungen zum jüdisch-christlichen Dialogue.* Neukirchen-Vluyn: Neukirchener, 1976].

North, Eric M. *The Book of a Thousand Tongues, Being Some Account of the Translation and Publication of All or Part of the Holy Scriptures into More Than a Thousand Languages and Dialects with Over 1100 Examples from the Text.* New York: Harper & Bros. for the American Bible Society, 1938.

Pick, Bernard. "Hebrew Versions of the New Testament." In *Cyclopedia of Biblical, Theological, and Ecclesiastical Literature*, edited by John McClintock and James Strong. New York: Harper, 1895 (and subsequently reprinted).

www.ingramcontent.com/pod-product-compliance
Lightning Source LLC
Chambersburg PA
CBHW050816160426
43192CB00010B/1788